HACKING
SCHOOL DISCIPLINE

HACKING
SCHOOL DISCIPLINE

9 WAYS TO CREATE
A **CULTURE** OF **EMPATHY**
& RESPONSIBILITY
USING **RESTORATIVE**
JUSTICE

HACK™
Learning
SERIES

NATHAN MAYNARD
BRAD WEINSTEIN

Published by Times 10
Highland Heights, OH
Times10Books.com

Cover Design by Steven Plummer
Interior Design by Steven Plummer
Editing by Carrie White-Parrish
Proofreading by Jennifer Jas

Library of Congress Cataloging-in-Publication Data is available.
ISBN: 978-1-948212-13-7
First Printing: March, 2019

For all those students who heard, "You aren't in trouble. I just need to talk to you." This is for you.

CONTENTS

INTRODUCTION
WHY DO WE NEED RESTORATIVE JUSTICE IN SCHOOLS?

CCORDING TO THE Civil Rights Data Collection, of the 49 million students enrolled in public schools in 2011–2012, 3.5 million were suspended in-school, 3.45 million were suspended out-of-school, and 130,000 were expelled. Another concerning fact from this source is that black students are suspended and expelled three times as often as white students, and students with disabilities are suspended twice as often as their non-disabled peers. Zero-tolerance policies, which deliver harsh, predetermined punishments, are a root cause of many suspensions and expulsions in schools today, often affecting minority students the most.

Removing students from their educational setting instead of using alternative forms of discipline has many negative effects, including increasing the likelihood that students will enter the juvenile justice system or end up in prison, often referred to as the school-to-prison pipeline. In short, mishandling discipline can greatly affect a student's educational trajectory, or even more disheartening, the student's life. It is our duty as professional educators to realize that within every wrongdoing is a teachable moment. Further, we must take advantage of that moment rather than throwing it—and the student—out with the trash.

Every behavior is a form of communication—even behaviors that require disciplinary action. Our responsibility as professional educators is to try to understand those behaviors and, simply put, begin to do better with our behavior management systems. We need to combat the disproportionality in our discipline policies, noted above, by examining and implementing equitable practices.

So how exactly do we do that?

This book isn't going to be the instant gratification cure-all to classroom management. It *is* going to be a tool to help you maintain tranquility in your classroom, a climate of respect, and a completely controlled culture using proven and effective methods of addressing problem behavior. Restorative justice takes situations that otherwise might result in a student being removed from class, and instead presents ways to teach the student how to repair the harm that was done, and continue forward. This method creates an atmosphere of communication and collaboration around student issues.

Every day is a new chance to connect with

your most difficult students. They are used to people giving up on them, and even blaming them when things go wrong. While it is important to hold students accountable, it is even more important to find the root cause of those difficult behaviors and address them. Let them know that you are there to help them, even if that means tough love. Wear them down with relentless kindness and encouragement. Never hold a grudge. A core idea of restorative practices is that students are not inherently troubled. Something has happened to cause that trouble. As teachers, we must dive into behavior as we do any learning deficiency in the classroom. In this case, the old mantra of carrot-and-stick discipline doesn't address the problem. Instead, it actually creates more opposition, exclusion, and labeling.

We must learn to go beyond that and truly change behavior—for both teachers and students.

Restorative practice is an emerging social science that studies how we can strengthen relationships between individuals, as well as social connections within communities. According to the International Institute of Restorative Practices (IIRP), "All humans are hardwired to connect. Just as we need food, shelter, and clothing, human beings also need strong and meaningful relationships to thrive." IIRP also says the use of restorative practices helps to:

- Reduce crime, violence, and bullying
- Improve human behavior
- Strengthen civil society
- Provide effective leadership
- Restore relationships
- Repair harm

We wrote this book based on more than twenty-five years of educational leadership experience and formal training from IIRP, with one goal: to teach you more about restorative discipline so you can use it to make a difference in students' lives. We'll show you how to use restorative practices to manage behaviors that would often result in punishment. Our exercises will demonstrate an alternate route made up of creating responsibility for actions, an obligation to repair the harm caused, and action steps for righting the wrong. This philosophy takes a deeper dive into the "why" behind a behavior, and seeks to create positive collaboration around issues, shared investments in the school climate, and healthy relationships among all stakeholders.

Emotional regulation isn't instinctive; it's learned.

A huge factor of both teacher and administrator job dissatisfaction—we would even say the bane of our existences—is dealing with challenging student behaviors. According to the Primary Sources: 2012 report, more than half of all teachers wish they could spend less time disciplining students throughout the day. Time spent disciplining students takes away from the primary reason many of us went into teaching: to help kids learn and grow. According to Primary Sources: America's Teachers on the Teaching Profession, 68 percent of elementary teachers, 64 percent of middle school teachers, and 53 percent of high school teachers believe there has been an increase in negative behaviors since they began teaching.

With an ever-evolving society, easily accessible technology that distracts both students and parents, and a culture that seems to value sports and entertainment more than school, educators have a harder job than ever. Much to our chagrin, negative behaviors aren't going anywhere. We can either continue to do what we've always done to discipline students, though it has been shown to be increasingly less effective, or we can change. That's right, we said "we" can change. We need to change if we are going to reinvent the way students are disciplined. We need to teach learners how to behave, not through yelling or screaming (which obviously doesn't work anyway), but through respectful coaching and accountability. Children today are not the same as we were during our school years; the world they operate within is more complex, competitive, and accessible. Through the aid of technology, students are exploring and communicating constantly, without guidance from adults. The sooner we can accept that and change with them, the better.

This does not mean we need to accept disrespect and other negative behaviors. It means we need to combat them in a different way.

We hope that this book will lay down the foundation to help you do that. Following, you'll find nine Hacks that will guide you on your path to restorative justice. Each Hack contains exercises, further descriptions, and examples following the format of other books in the *Hack Learning Series*. Each chapter presents easy-to-follow strategies under these section headings: The Problem, The Hack, What You Can Do Tomorrow, A Blueprint for Full Implementation, Overcoming Pushback, and The Hack in Action.

You might wonder why we would write an entire book on discipline, and the reason is simple. We believe it directly correlates with academic achievement.

With the help of responsible and caring discipline, we believe all schools can become physically and emotionally safer—which will help us launch our students into healthier and more productive lives. Every student deserves teachers who care for them. Restorative justice is the first step toward providing that.

HACK 1

LET'S TALK
CREATE A CULTURE OF COMMUNICATION TO RESOLVE CONFLICT

Rules without relationships inspire rebellion.
—JOSH MCDOWELL, AUTHOR OR CO-AUTHOR OF MORE
THAN 150 BOOKS, INCLUDING *RIGHT FROM WRONG*

THE PROBLEM: STUDENTS ARE NOT BEING HEARD

EDUCATORS DON'T ALWAYS give students a voice when they make a mistake. Punitive systems require that blame be assigned to one party, and punishment be given to address the behavior. However, punitive consequences mean creating a temporary bandage for an issue. They do very little when it comes to unveiling the full story and bringing all the issues to the forefront. A student punched another student and as a result, she is suspended. We may ask her, "What did you do to cause this problem? What are you going to do differently next time?" But those questions don't give her a voice in the issue. They don't even ask her why she did what she did. The line of questioning is a regular routine, and little more than a set of boxes—to which students have scripted answers.

It's no wonder so many students become repeat offenders. We aren't taking the time to get to the bottom of the issue, and that means that we aren't treating the cause. We're so busy following a routine that we forget to treat the students themselves.

This carrot-and-stick discipline does not cause lasting changes. It's an immediate response to a behavior, and often leads to a *forced* change in behavior. If you want a rabbit to get into a hole, you smack it with a stick. You can also use motivation and dangle a carrot over the opening until the rabbit is tricked and falls into the hole. But neither of these teaches the rabbit the value of going into the hole. Neither method makes the rabbit actually *want* to go into the hole. Further, both tactics are a bit unfair; the rabbit doesn't see the hole until he falls into it.

> BY SAYING "LET'S TALK" AND BY ASKING QUESTIONS, WE DEMONSTRATE THAT THIS MEETING IS NOT A PUNISHMENT; IT'S A CONVERSATION.

Likewise, our current systems either force or incentivize students to change. They don't teach the students the reason for the change—and they don't ask why the students were acting the way they were in the first place. Simply put, we must find a way to make students *want* the change, instead of forcing it on them. We need to hear what they're trying to tell us through their behavior, and use that to guide them in a different direction.

To achieve this objective, educators need to build relationships, create investment in the class climate, and give the students a voice— all of which can be accomplished through some simple Hacks.

THE HACK: LET'S TALK

We need to figure out how to hear student voices, rather than just using one-size-fits-all treatments for discipline. To do this, we need to seek to understand behaviors instead of just labeling them and assigning consequences. That means that immediately after a negative behavior occurs, we start with a series of open-ended questions:

- What happened?

- What were you thinking about when _____ happened?

- Who did this affect, and how so?

Once you understand more about the behavior, you can take the next step into the restorative discipline process. A restorative mediation is one way to deal with conflict in a constructive, supportive forum, with the goal of creating a resolution that addresses every aspect of the situation.

The mediation is fairly simple in process, but it might take a bit of practice to master. Here are the basics:

1. Identify the behavior that occurred.

2. Ask the involved student(s) to either step into the hallway for a quick conversation or to stay for a minute after class—whichever method makes more sense in your environment.

3. Use the open-ended questions listed above to learn more about the behavior and the reasons it happened.

4. Guide the conversation toward a meaningful and positive resolution.

By saying "Let's talk" and by asking questions, we demonstrate that this meeting is not a punishment; it's a conversation. As teachers, we want to give the students involved an opportunity to share their version of what happened, so all voices are heard.

According to the International Institute of Restorative Practices, effective responses to conflict, wrongdoing, and harm are the hallmark of restoring behaviors. By addressing the behavior immediately, allowing students to speak, and seeking to understand the situation, we keep from doling out quick punishments that might mishandle the situation. We also build an environment in which students understand what they did and why it was wrong, and help to build their own sets of consequences.

Mediation plays an important role in this process because you, as the leader, need to umpire the conversation to make sure it comes to a harmonious resolution. The core values of a restorative mediation (all beginning with the letter "r") illuminate the steps an educator or mediator should take when preparing an effective mediation.

- **RESPECT** is the foundation of a positive mediation experience. If all parties are interested in repairing the problem, they must respect one another's insights and emotions throughout this process.

- **RELATIONSHIPS** are the next step. Allow students to tell their side of the story so they learn to communicate and hear one another. A student may be surprised to hear that the other student might have lashed out because her grandmother recently passed away, and knowing that changes opinions. Human issues are usually relatable, and relationships can be built through that common understanding.

- **RESPONSIBILITY** means both parties involved in negative behaviors need to own their actions and consequences to move forward. See the following steps for ideas on how to brainstorm meaningful and logical consequences as a team.

- **REPAIRING THE HARM** asks us as facilitators to get creative. Instead of just suspending students or assigning detentions, mediators must brainstorm tactics that will genuinely restore balance to the situation. If a student called his teacher a derogatory name, perhaps he could write a letter of apology after school hours. If two students teased another student on a public online forum, lead them toward a meaningful resolution. (Perhaps they would be interested in writing at least five positive social media posts about their peer.) Repairing the harm takes the entire team's agreement, though the facilitator will need to pave the way through creative thinking.

- **REINTEGRATING** the student or students into their normal routine after this meeting should be handled with respect and care. Offer to check in on them the next day, or ask if they need to take a short walk to clear their minds before returning to class. When students act out, it's not always easy to swallow their pride and return to business as usual. That return to normal life must be part of the equation for the mediation to work.

Holding students directly and personally responsible for their behavior is what sparks intrinsic change. Mediations give students insight into the real impact of their behavior. Combine them with restorative practices and you have the formula for empathy, positive culture, and lasting change.

WHAT YOU CAN DO TOMORROW

Though it may not feel that way after digesting these steps, mediations can be quick. You must set the tone and expectations, make sure that all parties have accepted wrongdoing, develop a plan for what happens next, and that's it! We recommend taking time to sit down and draw up your plans for future mediations so you're ready to handle situations like this when they happen. Until then, try these tactics to run a mediation the next time a behavior occurs:

- **FACILITATE THE MEDIATION.** Welcome all parties to the mediation and thank them for coming. This sets a positive tone right from the beginning. Use open-ended questions to guide the conversation. Instead of saying, "Did you think kicking over the trash can was a good decision?" ask "What was happening before you kicked over the trash can?" You want to target feelings and learn what has been going on. Mediations are your way to play detective and listen until you feel all appropriate discoveries have been brought to the surface. You can usually enhance the conversation by using affirmations when you hear something new. "Wow, thanks for sharing that. That must have been tough." Giving that feedback opens up the pipeline of the conversation.

- **ASSIGN A PLAN OF ACTION**. What are the next steps for each party after the mediation? How are you, as a collective team, going to prevent similar situations from occurring in the future? As the facilitator, you should summarize the facts of the event, emphasizing the pitfalls. Focus on developing future consequences together: if "this" happens again, "this" is what the consequence will be. Having the entire group's buy-in will help everyone feel accountable. Share reminders about school and class expectations. "We are in this together; let's have each other's backs."

- **INFORM AS NEEDED**. Who in the student's life should be brought into the discussion? Who considers themselves to be stakeholders in the student's success? Which cheerleader would benefit from a summary of the mediation? Consider groups that are already invested in the learners: parents, other teachers, school counselors, athletic coaches, probation officers, board members, and so on. Don't complain to these people, but instead praise the journey of how the student is working to repair the harm. This is especially helpful if you uncovered underlying stress or trauma that might continue to affect the student's behavior, as this knowledge can help an adult honor the student's story and respond sensitively in future situations.

- **RECORD THE DETAILS.** Recording the behavior, mediation, and plan of action allows you to analyze trends in behavior, track recidivism, and create a holistic profile of the students' journeys. This can include a summary of the session, such as: "To summarize what we discussed here today, Tyrone is going to apologize to Mrs. Maylee tomorrow before class begins. I am going to check in with him at the end of that class and ensure this reparation occurred." Summarizing the mediation before dismissing the group helps to ensure that everyone understands what was said during the conference, and also reminds the participants how the harm will be repaired, maintaining the restorative tone from the beginning to the end of the mediation.

- **PREPARE THE FACILITY.** Use restorative language throughout the building, classrooms, and hallways through everyday speech. Down the road, consider creating appealing and easy-to-read signage. Use this language not just with students but with staff in all settings. Examples may include:

- Our Restorative Core Values are respect, relationships, responsibility, repair, and reintegration.
- Remember the five R's: Respect | Relationships | Responsibility | Repair | Reintegration
- RESPECT every person. Build RELATIONSHIPS with those around you. Take RESPONSIBILITY for your choices and actions. REPAIR situations quickly and honestly. REINTEGRATE into a routine.

- **EVALUATE.** Maintain an open dialogue with school staff to successfully implement the restorative culture shift. Staff should be able to openly discuss how adult behavior affects student interactions, and discuss possible effects of implicit bias. Be honest with one another. Hold meetings after a mediation. Leadership team members should be prepared to meet one-on-one with staffers who demonstrate potentially damaging behaviors.

A BLUEPRINT FOR FULL IMPLEMENTATION

While restorative mediations can be quick to execute, they might take a bit of practice to master. There is more to consider than you may think, so let's break down how to set yourself—and your students—up for a successful mediation experience.

STEP 1: Identify the conflict and the guilty party.

This is the step you must take before starting the mediation. Your goal is to identify what happened and who was affected, and have the offenders admit to their personal actions. A helpful tool for learning a student's perspective is recapping the student's personal account of what happened, and then moving on to a prompting question such as, "So you only looked at him once, and he threw a pencil at you?" This allows the student to slow down and realize there may be more to the story. You can also tell the students that the more information they provide, the sooner you will be done with the situation. We like to tell students that if they don't tell us everything, this won't be resolved, and there might be a consequence later if we find out more. This encourages them to own everything now, so we can bring closure to the situation and move on.

STEP 2: Invite all stakeholders to participate.

A stakeholder is anyone who participated in or was affected by the negative behavior. Example: James threw a pencil at Allen, hitting him in the back of the head. Allen started to yell at James and the entire class stopped reading to see what was going on. The stakeholders are: James (wrongdoer), Allen (victim), the entire class (all witnessed the outburst made by the victim after he was hit by the pencil), and the teacher (who had to stop teaching and address the situation). You then must decide who should be part of this mediation. Do not feel like you have to include every stakeholder, but include everyone who had an important role.

STEP 3: Communicate the goals and values.

Students and all participants need to know the mediation's purpose. The goals are the core values, as covered earlier, and should provide the map for the mediation's forward movement. Write these goals on a board or pad of paper and set them out so everyone can see them, to make sure they figure into the mediation. It's also a good idea to come to a consensus regarding the end goal of the mediation.

STEP 4: Create a safe and supportive environment.

Set the mediation up for success by assigning seats, taking into consideration personalities, and using strategies to decrease the anxiety of all stakeholders. Start by establishing the tone of the conversation, communicating expectations for behavior during the mediation, and summarizing the goals of the session. We like to place our most volatile or emotionally driven student closest to the door. Have you heard it said that you should never corner a wasp, or you will get stung? If you try to put the most volatile student in the corner, you will see why!

As the facilitators, we also like to try to keep the environment as calm as possible: no technological devices visible, noise and distractions at a minimum, and in a private setting. If a peer can walk past and see the mediation, it can cause anxiety in the attendees, which will take away from the progress you have built.

It's a good idea to let everyone know that there's a way to put the mediation on pause, as well. Let your students know that if they become upset during the mediation, their feelings will be honored. They have the option of getting up and walking out of the mediation. Assign a specific destination and length of time for the break so students know exactly what to do during the break and how long it will last. Example: "If you become upset, you can walk out of the office and sit right outside the office for one minute. After a minute, I will check on you and invite you to come back in. If you can't come back in, that's fine, but I will end the mediation. If the mediation ends unsuccessfully, the consequence will be out of your hands, and I will have to dictate what happens."

STEP 5: Recap and share perspective.

If students are going to learn, you need to give them a voice to tell their perspective of what happened, and discuss their feelings about it. This is just-the-facts storytelling. If a student gets off-task and states something like, "She started looking at me like she wanted to fight," reframe with, "You mean she was looking at you. We don't know if she wanted to fight until she tells us her side of the story. Now, please keep telling us what happened." Once both students go through their separate accounts of what happened, it's time for non-confrontational questions. You can lead these questions, or you can open it up to whomever was involved.

Make sure that all parties raise their hands, and that only one speaks at a time. Once emotions get involved with the storytelling component, it's easy to lose sight of the goals of the mediation. To stay on track, encourage them to ask non-accusatory questions that seek to understand what happened. Instead of saying, "Did you want to fight me?" the student should reframe that question as, "What was your intention looking at me? Was anything else going on?" This takes emotion out and keeps the conversation in the upper level of thinking.

After all students tell their stories and the group comes up with a generally subjective perspective of what happened, summarize what you discussed.

STEP 6: Repair and reinforce positivity.

Now that you have identified what happened and taken out the assumptions, you can delve into repairing the damage. Sometimes a situation can be resolved simply by figuring out the real story and dispelling the assumptions that a student had due to past interactions or misinterpretation. If this clarity does not provide resolution, take steps toward uncovering what the victim wants to happen moving forward. This can be anything from letters of apology, apologizing in the conference, and/or other ways to make the wrong right. We will dive more into this in Hack 3 (Repair the Harm).

It's a good idea to establish the plan of action moving forward, as this will help keep the behavior from happening again. You want the students to come up with this, however. Example: "If you have a question about what I was looking at or thought I had a problem, I want you to ask me in person." Reinforce positive statements from the students, and encourage positive action plans.

STEP 7: Build therapeutic rapport.

Now it's time to reintegrate and move forward. Stress the importance of relationships and the joy of being able to resolve the conflict in such a positive manner. The more students go through restorative mediations, the more positivity will start to reign in your classroom.

OVERCOMING PUSHBACK

Mediations take patience, and have to be looked at as investments. The skills used in the mediations can be multi-purposed and incorporated in other areas of the students' lives. That doesn't mean that everyone will understand them—or their importance. Following are examples of the pushback you might receive from both teachers and students.

THIS ISN'T MY JOB. Student success *is* your job, no matter what role you play in the school. A successful school culture starts with relationships and focuses on participation and investment from all, especially during a conflict. Spending time cultivating conflict resolution tools based on open communication is a win-win for everyone.

WHERE CAN I FIND THE TIME? Before class, after class, during students' lunch, or the next day (you don't want to let it lie for too long, but do your best with what you have) are all reasonable solutions for this pushback. The more time you dedicate to creating successful students who feel heard, the easier your job will be. Chances are, if you do not dedicate the time up front to fully resolve a conflict, offer closure, and create a plan to prevent repeated behaviors, you will end up spending more time on this same issue again in the future. Mediations are investments that offer amazing results.

THIS WON'T WORK. You might think, "My students will just fake all of this. They won't mean it, and nothing will change!" In reality, they could. It doesn't have to be that way, though, and you have influence over student buy-in. This is why you don't want to lead with closed questions like, "Are you mad?" or "Are you going to do this again?" Change them to, "How are you feeling right now?" or

"What do you think would happen in the future if you talked with her first?" We have practiced mediations like that for a decade, and can tell you that it's hard for students to fake it in front of their enemies or the persons they offended. Target feelings, and when you hear them, give the students praise and affirmations. Encourage the communication! It won't flow right away, but be patient. Once you hit that target, you'll get buy-in from the students, and change will happen.

THE HACK IN ACTION

During a passing period, Maddie hurried into class right before the bell rang. She opened up her laptop, and I heard an uproar of laughter. Maddie looked back and Devon was glaring at her and smirking. I quickly redirected and previewed the expectations of the class.

"Today as we explore types of cells, I am sure we will all uphold the classroom norms by engaging productively in work, maintaining a safe and clean environment, and sharing the space effectively. Let's have a great class!"

I continued with the lesson for about fifteen minutes before I heard, "Girl, you think this is cute?"

I turned around and saw Maddie walking toward Devon, who was still sitting down. Devon started to stand up, but Maddie shoved her. I ran back toward the rear of the class, but it was too late. This situation ended after about two minutes of punches being thrown, yelling, desks flipping, and me getting hit in the chest.

After the girls were separated, I asked the dean to escort them down to the office. I immediately said, "circle up," to my other students, and we all pulled our chairs in the shape of a circle. This was a way for me to give them an outlet to process what happened, reduce some anxiety, and reset the classroom climate. Without that, we wouldn't be able to do any learning. I pulled out the classroom's talking piece (which can be anything easy to pass or toss around the room, such as a small stuffed animal or squishy ball) and started by saying, "I'm disappointed. This is not how we deal with conflicts, and I'm sorry we all had to be a part of that." We continued to go around the circle, with different students volunteering to talk about the conflict that took place, until we decided to close the circle and restart the lesson. In the meantime, Devon and Maddie's parents were called to take them home for the day.

After class, I spoke with the dean to organize the mediation. We scheduled a meeting thirty minutes before school started, and arranged to have both students in prior to reintegrating them back into the class. I spoke to each student separately on the phone to discuss the incident. They both agreed that what they did was not the way to handle conflict, and were both open to the mediation to help "squash the beef." I incentivized their participation, with the support of the dean, by promising that if the mediation was successful, they could return to class. If they were not successful in the mediation, they would have to finish their second day of out-of-school suspension. The mediation was a way for them to only serve the first day away from school and repair the harm, in place of a second day of suspension.

Maddie and Devon both showed up bright and early at 7:30 a.m., before the first bell rang at 8:15 a.m. I had Maddie sit closest to the door, knowing that she was the more historically emotional student. I started the conference by saying: "I appreciate you both being here to squash this together. What happened yesterday was unacceptable, and I do not want this to happen again. I want you both to know that if you get upset during this mediation, you can walk out. You will be permitted to sit alone on the bench outside of the classroom for two minutes. After two minutes, you will need to re-enter the mediation, if you feel prepared. If you do not, we won't continue. You will then have to serve the second day of out-of-school suspension. Also, I need mutual respect being given at all times. At the end of the day, I want you to know that I am in charge of this mediation. We will have only one person speak at a time; if you want to speak, you will raise your hand. Everyone is going to be given a voice during this mediation, as I want to hear from every single person involved in this incident. You must both accept that if this mediation is not successful, you will have to serve your second day of suspension prior to re-entering the class. Do you both understand?"

After a pause for agreement, I continued with: "Okay, Maddie you start first. Please tell me what has been going on with you and Devon. Start as far back as you can remember when the beef started happening."

Maddie said that the issues had started when Devon posted a story on Snapchat about her. The Snapchat story said, "It's not second helpings. It's main helpings." Maddie said she knew it was about her, and so she said something. They went back and forth on Snapchat, arguing, name-calling, and talking about fighting. Maddie also mentioned that she used to date a young man named Tyrell until he broke up with her for Devon.

Maddie then reached her emotional peak and said, "We used to be cool. I just don't know why you think it's okay to rub dating Tyrell in my face like that!"

Devon tried to speak, but I reminded her to raise her hand first, in order to be respectful of the mediation process. Devon raised her hand and was called on.

"I just don't like you still trying to talk to him," Devon said. "I saw that you and him still talk. I'm not dumb."

"No, he talks to me," Maddie responded. "I just reply to him. You must not have read what he was saying."

She and Devon then began to discuss what was being said and how they felt about it. This was exactly what I was going for: open dialogue with feelings.

Ten minutes later, I stated, "Wow, this is all over a misunderstanding on Snapchat? I'm glad you two can finally talk about this. Do you have anything else that has been bothering you that you want to talk about?"

Maddie raised her hand. "I just want to know why you, Lindsey, Claire, and Rebecca were all laughing at me."

Devon laughed and said, "What?! No. We weren't laughing at you. Lindsey just showed us a picture of Geoff. That dude is always creeping on her!"

They both laughed at that.

I brought us back to the goals of the mediation by saying, "Great job today. I want to ask again, is there anything else anyone wants to say? If not, let's be done with this and move forward."

Maddie said, "Well, I'm sorry. I shouldn't have said that stuff on Snapchat, and wish it hadn't gone this far."

Devon, with a tear in her eye, mumbled, "Me too. I'm sorry. For real. This is all stupid."

I quickly summarized what we discussed and finished by saying that this meant the situation was finished. I also stressed that if a situation came up between them in the future, the two of them needed to communicate. I reviewed several suggestions on how to communicate and also added insight on how being a keyboard warrior didn't help things. Finally, I asked them who exactly had seen the fight.

Devon said, "Everyone."

I said, "Yes, the entire class did see this. How do you think it could have affected them, Maddie?"

She stated, "They were probably scared that we could have run into them. Maybe mad that we messed up the class."

"For sure. I agree with you, and it's good that you can identify that. So what can we do to repair the harm with the entire class?" I asked.

Devon and Maddie then came up with the talking points and agreed to speak to the class and apologize for the altercation. We also discussed how they might apologize to their instructor for disrupting the lesson.

These two girls never fought again, and they ended up being close friends afterward. The mediation ended with tears, like most do. It's good to target the feelings and empathy of everyone involved. Mediations take patience, and can't be forced. Once they are finished, though, you will understand why it was the right way to deal with the conflict.

Students can solve their own issues when you provide them with a constructive forum to do so, and mediations are that forum. Teach the students to keep relationships at the forefront of every decision, and run a mediation with open-ended, leading questions. Focus on empathy and praise emotional literacy to help the students learn how to handle conflict in positive ways, and remember to keep several foundational principles at the core of the mediations: identify what led to the behaviors, what has happened since the behaviors, and what underlying factors turned this issue into what it was.

CIRCLE UP
DEAL WITH THE ISSUE IMMEDIATELY AND WHERE IT HAPPENS

Divide each conflict into as many parts as feasible and necessary to resolve it.
—René Descartes, philosopher

THE PROBLEM: CLASSROOM ISSUES AREN'T BEING DEALT WITH IN THE CLASSROOM

CLASSROOM CLIMATE IS about finding a balance, and it depends on the relationships of everyone who is part of that class. Students must be accountable for their behavior and how it affects others. But when a student is removed from the classroom because of a negative behavior, he or she is no longer accountable for the impact the behavior had on the relationships with the class. Instead, the student begins to learn that the negative behavior is a way to get out of the classroom.

So what happens when a student doesn't want to read out loud?

She knows the way out. Or what happens if a student is embarrassed because his ex-girlfriend is still in the class? Yep, you guessed it. They know how to get out of that situation.

The negative behavior du jour can bring your lesson to a skidding halt and put you in a predicament. You are pressured to address the problem quickly and appropriately, with all eyes on you. The quickest and easiest solution is a referral to the office. After all, you have a whole class to teach, a new activity to pass out, emails to answer, and daily attendance to take. We all get it. But how can we expect our students to do any better *in the classroom* if we just remove them when they do something wrong?

When the student returns from his field trip to the office or from in-school suspension, the behavior has been addressed, but the relationship has not. There may still be tension between the student and the teacher or the student and the classmates. You haven't addressed any harm the student might have caused to the class as a whole, and that leaves the classroom climate damaged. The entire class is still sitting on the edge of a knife, and will be distracted by the tension.

The answer? Fix it—*within the classroom*. And to make sure it sticks, involve the entire class.

THE HACK: CIRCLE UP

The first thing that we as teachers need to do is to stop offering students the easy way out through removal from class. Many school districts maintain a goal of keeping the students in the classroom, where they're adding to and taking advantage of the learning experience. When kids are in class, we see higher attendance rates, increased test scores, and positive climates. That goes away the second we send kids to the principal's office for misbehaving.

Instead of giving them that out, seek new ways of handling bad behavior, including classroom circles. These circles allow you to enforce the classroom expectations without losing one of your community members.

As you might expect, circles are gatherings in which all participants sit in a circular shape facing each other to facilitate open, direct communication. Circles provide a safe and supportive space where everyone can talk freely about sensitive topics, work through differences, and build consensus. Best of all, circles invite shared power and responsibility.

Circles don't have to be used only during times of conflict, either. Start your class with a "check-in circle" as a great way to begin the day, and invite students to share their feelings and listen to others.

- Have all the students sit in a circle.

- Teachers should include themselves in the circle to signal that they are facilitators and listeners during these gatherings, not authority figures.

- Start with a check-in question, such as "What's one interesting thing you read online yesterday?"

- Add mindfulness exercises to help release tension and build focus on the present moment.

  - **MINDFUL BREATHING**. Ask students to breathe in through their noses and out through their mouths for six seconds. Instruct them to purposefully pay attention to their breath and heart rate as they continue to breathe slowly in and out.

- **MINDFUL AWARENESS.** Ask the students to look around the room and think about what they are grateful for today. Is it cold outside, making it wonderful to be inside with the heat? Does the lighting fill the classroom with enough light to see each other? How does the hand sanitizer help everyone maintain health? Giving students a few moments to reconnect with the world around them might help them settle into the circle and start the day with positivity.

- **MINDFUL APPRECIATION.** Have students take turns sharing things that they appreciate about their lives. Leading questions include, "What are you thankful for today? Who has inspired you recently? What are you proud of accomplishing this week?" When learners pause and reflect on their positives, the transition into a positive classroom culture becomes easier to achieve.

- Devote at least five minutes to circle time each morning, and gradually expand as students get more comfortable, or decrease the time if you have other items on your agenda that take priority.

- Always allow students to opt out if they choose. Remember that restorative practices center around respect.

Restorative circles can also be useful tools when you're trying to address specific issues or concerns in the classroom.

- Tell students to "circle up," just like you do during morning check-in circles.

- Include yourself in the circle to signal that you are a facilitator and listener rather than an authority figure.

- As the facilitator, identify the key factors in the conflict or classroom issue.

- Set the climate of the room and go over your expectations. Example: "No cell phones, and only talk when you have the talking piece. Right now we are focusing on the distractions that were happening in the classroom while I was teaching. Who wants to start?"

- Once students start sharing what bothers them about the issue or behavior, ask additional follow-up questions to the group, such as, "How did that make you feel?" or "Why did the pencil being thrown upset you?" Give students the opportunity to hold one another accountable, discuss ways to repair the harm, and continue on with the day.

- Once comments become repetitive or begin dying down, it's time to end the circle.

- Before the restorative circle is finished, discuss the next steps and review the solution your students have decided on.

- Ask students to dissolve the circle, meaning they quickly return their chairs to classroom position.

- Provide a preview and reset of classroom expectations before moving back into the lesson plan.

PRO TIP: Wrap circles (to wrap-up issues at the end of class) are great for experienced circle-up instructors and classroom communities. Once you and your students have mastered circles, begin allowing students to call their own circles to "clear the air" on issues that you might not be aware of. Use the following guidelines to structure your student-led wrap circles:

- Students are allowed to call wrap circles any day of the week, and within the last five minutes of class only.

- The student who calls the circle becomes the facilitator, with the instructor still a part of the group to help guide the discussion and maintain the expectations.

- Once the student shares a grievance with the group, ask others to comment on it. Candy says, "It's lame that someone stole my folder. It has important papers I need for my business." Another student says, "Yeah, my earbuds were stolen, too. My mom paid good money for those, and I need them back."

- Push forward toward a solution and ask others in the circle how you can all help eliminate these behaviors. "We need to have each other's backs. If

CIRCLES ARE A POWERFUL WAY TO ALLOW THE STUDENTS TO ADDRESS AN ISSUE AS A COLLECTIVE VOICE. THEY CAN BE USED TO START THE DAY OFF IN A POSITIVE WAY, OR REINFORCE POSITIVE COMMUNICATION FOR CONFLICT RESOLUTION.

you see something, say something." Another student adds, "Okay, like how I think I saw your folder with Hannah. Did you let her borrow it?"

- Before the class ends, the circle must be closed. Facilitators should review the concerns and solutions.

- The next day, preview and reset classroom expectations, or add the topic into the check-in circle for closure.

WHAT YOU CAN DO TOMORROW

Circles are a powerful way to allow the students to address an issue as a collective voice. They can be used to start the day off in a positive way, or reinforce positive communication for conflict resolution. Start building the plans for your own in-class circles or call your first circle using the following steps.

- **CREATE A SAFE PLACE.** Students should be able to sit face-to-face in a circle, either at their desks or in free-standing chairs, and should feel safe doing so—and safe in the circle itself. Establish right away that this is a no-judgment zone; there will be no assumptions or subjective statements, and the students can feel physically safe. If students violate any of these expectations, they will be removed from the circle. You will be amazed

by how effective this is! Students quickly learn
how empowering it is to be part of a circle.
(Helpful tip: In a potentially physical situation, a
circle won't work. Jump back to the mediation
section.)

- **ESTABLISH EXPECTATIONS.** Use a "talking piece" as
  the identifier for the person who currently holds
  the floor. This keeps everyone from talking
  at once. Set strict guidelines for "facts only"
  talk. Tell students that they can openly discuss
  issues, but only if they use affirmative "I" statements. See Hack 6 (Teach Mindfulness).

- **PROMOTE COMMUNICATION.** Praise open dialogue
  and productive conversations, and thank anyone
  who feels comfortable enough to share. Example:
  "Wow, that must have been tough to admit in
  front of everyone that you feel embarrassed
  coming into class sometimes. Thank you for letting us know. I appreciate you." Positivity often
  leads to engagement.

- **PRAISE EMPATHY.** Praise any student who demonstrates empathy, to help build appreciation
  for it. When students can recognize emotions,
  their emotional literacy goes up and this helps
  them build a circle that cultivates empathy.
  This also trains students how to use empathy in
  other situations.

- **WRAP UP THE CIRCLE.** When you feel the discussion has come to a natural end, recap what happened and describe the next steps if you've discussed and decided on an action plan for repairing the harm. Thank everyone for their participation. A quick reminder of the sense of community within your class is always a great closing remark.

A BLUEPRINT FOR FULL IMPLEMENTATION

This blueprint is about more than just implementing a quick circle, and moves toward creating circles as the way you deal with situations.

STEP 1: Make restorative circles the norm.

In addition to modeling the behavior you want and rewarding positive behavior through affirmations, use the circles to build a habit in your classroom. Students should know exactly what to expect when the class needs to address a negative behavior or conflict, and this creates a foundation for addressing these problems.

STEP 2: Call the circle.

You started the activity with a preview of your expectations. You redirected a negative behavior, and you issued a consequence. If the issue still isn't resolved, it's time to move into a circle.

- **CALL FOR STUDENTS TO "CIRCLE UP."** Students should know that this means you want them to grab their chairs and form a circle. In the beginning, the teacher should be the only one who can call a circle. Down the road, you can empower students to call circles to hold one another accountable.

- **SET TIME LIMITS.** You want to establish an appropriate amount of time for addressing an incident. If you don't put boundaries on the timeline, students might use circles to avoid getting back to work, and conversations will not be as productive. Determine the time limit based on the flow of your class and the severity of the incident, but try to aim for between two and ten minutes.

- **TALK THROUGH THE PROBLEM.** Use the talking piece to discuss the issue at hand. Use the strategies above to encourage respectful conversation and solution-oriented thinking.

- **REVIEW ACTION ITEMS.** The last part of the circle is to talk about what will happen when moving forward. Does one particular student need to clean up a mess, write a letter of apology, or stay after school to organize classroom supplies? If the issue is classroom-wide, then the action item will be, too. Does the teacher now need to establish a seating chart? Having the entire class involved in the discussion means you also have them involved in the solution— and that they're buying in to the responsibility of enforcing that solution.

STEP 3: Follow up.

The circle established what the student needs to do in order to repair the harm. Summarize the key points and plan of action, and then thank your class for their involvement. Thanking the class for their commitment to the classroom climate helps to build respect and community. After the circle has ended, reset the classroom expectations in a preview. Example: "Remember, we are going to be jumping back into reviewing compound sentences. I need cell phones put away and everyone to open up their books once they go back to their seats." You might still need to assign a consequence, per your classroom norms, for the student or students who acted out. Do this at the end of class in a one-on-one conversation.

OVERCOMING PUSHBACK

Circles are part of the "invisible hand" classroom monitoring system. The payment for having this luxury service isn't instantaneous or free. It takes an investment of time and energy—and you'll almost inevitably experience pushback on putting in that time.

CIRCLES TAKE AWAY FROM LESSON TIME. Yes, they do. It's by far the largest con of holding a circle. The great thing is that you are in charge of when they occur. You can call an audible to get the class back on track, like "ELMO" (Enough, Let's Move On), or simply pause. Circles are truly a classroom power move. Initially, you'll invest time to establish the practice, but that dissipates as students master it. As a teacher, you have to weigh your priorities and determine whether or not it is worth the time it will take to facilitate a circle. It's about finding the perfect ratio for you and your class. If you start them, circles will eventually become a natural part of your classroom climate, and behaviors will start fixing themselves.

You will start noticing students giving the patented "teacher stare-down" to their fellow misbehaving students, and negative behaviors will stop without your involvement. It's like magic!

THIS TAKES TOO LONG. Investment in classroom climates and school cultures doesn't pay off overnight. The time you put into facilitating a circle is advantageous to your climate, the students, and the number of redirections you will have to do *in the future*. We normally start the school year using one to two restorative circles per week. By the end of the first quarter, we've seen the use of circles go down to one every other week, and then even less. The proof is in the pudding; a reduced need for restorative circles shows that students learn from this process and don't continue the unwanted behaviors.

ISN'T THIS A COLLECTIVE PUNISHMENT? This is a collective investment into building culture. It invites shared power into misbehavior, creating a strong sense of classroom community. The classroom community promotes self-responsibility and effective action after a circle takes place. Instead of viewing it as a punishment, frame it as an opportunity for all students to be heard and for behaviors to improve.

THE HACK IN ACTION

Mr. Maynard's back is to the class when a pencil zips past his head. He turns around and notices that James has a guilty look on his face. Mr. Maynard considers kicking James out of the classroom. The pencil almost hit him, after all. James needs to learn his lesson. If Mr. Maynard lets James stay in the classroom, by Tuesday he's going to see half the class making it rain highlighters. He has to address this quickly and firmly.

Just as Mr. Maynard is about to address the class, a student named Julia says, "circle up," and the class quickly configures a makeshift circle with their chairs. "Sarah, will you be the timekeeper? We have two minutes," Julia begins, as she grabs the squishy happy-face stress ball the class has established as the all-powerful talking piece. She then begins the circle discussion. "I don't know who threw the pencil, but I feel upset when I almost get hit when I'm trying to listen. I don't like math, but I know I need to figure it out. Who is responsible for the damage?"

A few students sheepishly look toward James, who lowers his head.

Another talkative student zestfully raises his hand, catches the stress ball, and says, "I feel upset that Mr. Maynard just about got hit with a pencil. That's not cool."

A few more students add to the conflict-resolution circle, and after two minutes, Sarah says, "Time! What's the action step?"

Julia says, "I think if anyone throws a pencil, he should write a letter of apology to Mr. Maynard and one for every student in the class. Is that okay, Mr. Maynard?"

Mr. Maynard replies, "Sounds good. Let's jump back into these exciting polynomials."

The students return their chairs to their desks and Mr. Maynard returns to his lesson. After class, Mr. Maynard follows up with James.

"Hey, buddy. One of our classroom norms is to maintain a safe and clean environment. Throwing that pencil definitely wasn't in line with our norms. The consequence is that you will get five behavior points. Remember that you also need to repair the harm you caused by writing your letters of apology. Let's have those ready to hand out by Monday."

James nods and continues on to his next class. The next morning, he presents his letters of apology.

A restorative circle can be used to start the day off with positivity and to address a classroom issue in a safe environment to catalyze investment in change. It promotes relationships and the value of communication in a community forum. These circles are a supportive, not labeling, space where students can talk about sensitive topics, work through differences, and build consensus. Making them the norm in your classroom can reduce bad behaviors and increase empathy among the students.

HACK 3

REPAIR THE HARM
TEACH STUDENTS TO TAKE DIRECT
RESPONSIBILITY FOR THEIR ACTIONS

*Either we spend time meeting children's emotional
needs by filling their cup with love or we spend
time dealing with the behaviors caused from their
unmet needs. Either way we spend the time.*

—Pam Leo, author of *Connection Parenting*

THE PROBLEM: PUNITIVE
CONSEQUENCES DO NOT WORK

SUSPENSIONS, DETENTIONS, AND referrals to the office all
have one common flaw: they are exclusionary processes.
Asher threw pencil + Finlee threw pencil = two referrals
to the office. They are both removed from the class and
"taught" a lesson through the consequence. Throwing pencils =
referral to the office. What happens when Asher comes back to
class the next day after he missed the lesson because he was in the

49

office, and you give a pop quiz? Is he going to be able to conceptualize the skills he never learned, and do well on the quiz? Or is he going to recall what happened the day before: "Oh, throwing pencils = I don't have to be in this class?" This might come as a surprise to you, but some students don't want to be in class. Those students quickly realize that traditional consequences will get them out of certain activities, and they can abuse the system for their own purposes.

Why do students want to be excluded from class, or removed completely? It could be any combination of the following:

- Can't keep up with the lesson

- Relationship issues with peers or teacher

- Undiagnosed disorders that make it hard for them to concentrate

- Not feeling welcome or safe in the environment

- Feeling unwanted by the classroom climate

- Not engaged

- Boredom

- Negative emotions about a particular activity or subject

Traditional punitive systems also do very little teaching, and take very little thought. They barely even bother with student individuality. When something goes wrong, we immediately ask:

- What rule/law was broken?

- Who broke it?

- What punishment do they deserve?

From there, we have a list of possible punishments, the most serious of which is suspension. A suspension might help a student who broke a rule or expectation—but it might not.

POSITIVES OF SUSPENSIONS:

- Teaches a student that negative behavior has a consequence
- Removes the struggling student from the environment for a short time
- Reduces the classroom disruptions
- Alleviates classroom management pressure from the instructor

NEGATIVES OF SUSPENSIONS:

- Tends to support labeling of students
- Temporary bandage approach, with few lasting effects
- Victims get little from the process
- Little accountability
- Not typically a teaching tool
- Suspensions and expulsions place high-risk students out in the community, which could lead to higher dropout rates and criminal activities

Do the positives really outweigh the negatives? Or are we forcing all students into the same mold by doling out the same punishments regardless of student individuality? Traditional punishments don't focus on the victims or the classroom climate of a negative behavior. They send a message that certain behavior isn't tolerated, but Asher and Finlee are going to be coming back into that classroom. They are going to return from the suspension, and little will have changed. Consequences were given out for a negative behavior, but the harm has not been repaired for any of the other impacted parties. The students who were suspended learned that throwing pencils will get them out of class and then right back into it.

The consequence did not link to the behavior, and so the behavior will not change. If a consequence isn't logical (connected to the behavior) and the student is not emotionally invested in the effect of his behavior on others or the effect of the consequence on himself in the long-term, the consequence won't be effective (this is when the magic of empathy is needed). We need to find a different way to handle those consequences if we're to teach our students to stop misbehaving.

THE HACK: REPAIR THE HARM

Taking responsibility for behavior is the foundation of every restorative action. These actions are given to students to repair the harm they caused, and should directly relate to that harm. For example, if a student throws food in the lunchroom, he or she could have a restorative action of cleaning the lunchroom after school.

Creating restorative justice is simple, effective, and improves the school climate. Involving students in that creation allows them to take personal responsibility for the situation, and buy into the consequence.

When we're seeking to repair the harm, we start by posing two questions: To whom was the harm caused? How are you going to repair the harm? The students must come up with what they want to say or do as a consequence, and be willing participants in serving that consequence. You can do this by giving the student two options:

1. You can come up with the solution with me, or

2. I can come up with what your consequence will be, and I'm not going to be open to feedback.

This normally drives the student to want to be a part of the consequence, and to have an investment in it.

Restorative practices are effective because they turn every conflict into a learning opportunity. Instead of just labeling a negative behavior and assigning an automatic consequence, it seeks to understand the behavior. This, in turn, makes sure that together, you address every factor that could have played a part in the decision. This focuses on the need to repair the harm that has occurred. It also creates a sense of community in school, and restores damaged relationships by allowing all voices to be heard.

Another large component of why it is successful is that it helps students develop empathy by allowing the wrongdoer to hear exactly how the victim and/or stakeholders were affected by the behavior. It is powerful to have a student sit across from someone he hurt, own his behavior, and ask how to "fix it" (repair the harm). Most of the time, it ends with just an apology, but it opens up a respectful dialogue during which all students address the issue.

If students don't feel like they are being heard, they may refuse to buy into any consequence. Allowing them to help build those consequences, however, encourages them to take part in repairing the harm, and growing from the experience.

WHAT YOU CAN DO TOMORROW

If a student makes a mistake in the classroom, have the student come up with a consequence that will allow her to repair the harm done to other individuals, the classroom climate, or the school climate as a whole. This creates investment and the opportunity to develop problem-solving skills.

- **INITIATE.** Identify what harm the student caused and to whom. The first questions you might ask include:
    - *What happened?*
    - *Who has been affected by what you have done?*
- **EMPATHIZE.** Students have to take in others' perspectives to identify how they might have affected them. Use open-ended questions:
    - *How do you think they felt when ____ happened?*
    - *In what ways do you think ____ affected them?*
- **ANALYZE.** In the analyze phase, the student must create a way to repair the harm. It is important for the student to come up with this on his own, with

prompting. Try using these open-ended questions when designing a plan to make amends:

- *What do you think you need to do to make things right?*
- *How are you going to carry out this plan to repair the harm?*
- *How does this repair the harm that was done?*
- *Does it take care of everyone affected by the negative behavior?*

- **EXECUTE**. Carry out the solution you and the student created.

- **REFLECT**. This is when the student can collaborate with parents. Together, parents and the student can revisit the negative behavior and its impact on others, how the student came up with the solution to repair the harm, how the solution was carried out, and whether or not it truly repaired the harm. They should also discuss how the student felt about the process. In addition to speaking with the parents, help the student build a plan of action to prevent the negative behavior from happening again.

A BLUEPRINT FOR FULL IMPLEMENTATION

Use the following blueprint to break down this process from start to finish, and help students take responsibility for dealing with a problem behavior.

STEP 1: Delve into the behavior.

Start by approaching the issue in very black-and-white terms. "Asher, I saw you throw your pencil at Caleb from across the room. What were you thinking when you did that?" Ask open-ended questions while seeking to understand the behavior. When students open up or take responsibility, respond with affirmations. This provides positive encouragement for them to continue opening up about the situation. During this process, you might find that the students had something larger going on.

When we look at a behavior, we try to use the "iceberg perspective" and realize that every behavior has other things packed under it. You may just see the anger sticking out and think that's all that is going on. When you start to ask the open-ended questions and seek to understand, however, you may find other factors. For example, you know that Asher threw the pencil because he was mad. The iceberg perspective asks why he was mad. By asking open-ended questions, you might learn that he just found out that his girlfriend went to the movies with his best friend. His dad also recently moved out of his house, and his parents are in the midst of a messy divorce. His mom made him wear his least-favorite

> WHEN WE LOOK AT A BEHAVIOR, WE TRY TO USE THE "ICEBERG PERSPECTIVE" AND REALIZE THAT EVERY BEHAVIOR HAS OTHER THINGS PACKED UNDER IT.

shirt today because all his other clothes were dirty. He also has no clue how to do polynomials, and he "knows" he is going to fail the test next week.

Do these underlying reasons make it acceptable for him to throw a pencil at his peer? Absolutely not. But this knowledge does help you understand him not only as a student, but as a whole child.

Once you learn what was under Asher's iceberg, you can begin fostering change and restoring relationships and the school culture. You can address not only the specific choice of throwing a pencil at a classmate, but also take steps to reduce Asher's anxiety and connect him with resources to help him work through the factors that led to the behavior. If you hadn't taken the time to dive into the water and examine his iceberg, you never would have been able to address the root cause of the behavior and support him so that these behaviors do not continue.

STEP 2: Identify the stakeholders.

Once you understand the reasons for the behavior, you can help Asher make a change. Ask him to identify who he affected by throwing the pencil. It affected Asher himself; the other student, who threw a pencil in retaliation; the teacher who had to interrupt the lesson to address the flying utensils; the parents of both students, who now have to find out about this negative behavior; and the rest of the class, whose education this action interfered with.

This part is simple for us, as educators, but we want the students to identify all those people. The key to having the student identify the affected parties is to ask open-ended questions. Examples: Who did throwing the pencil affect? Who else? If others saw this, how could that have affected them? Keep digging until Asher lists everyone his actions affected.

You also want the students to identify how each stakeholder was affected. Lead the students through the continued use of open-ended questions, but don't give them the answers. The harder they think, the more effective this process will be. This is the cognitive component of empathy development: having the students step into someone else's perspective. This helps them develop empathy for what others were going through—and that empathy will stick out to them the next time they act.

STEP 3: Repair the harm.

This is the accountability and reparation component. Your next step is to make the wrong right, and repair the harm. Continue to guide the students in their decisions without telling them exactly how to proceed. Think of ways they could repair the harm, and guide them toward solutions through open-ended questions. Following is an example of a teacher and student deciding how to repair the harm with the class:

> The teacher, Mr. Wiley, states, "So you said the rest of the class saw you throw the pencil, and everyone laughed, and it stopped them from paying attention. So how could you fix this with the entire class?"
>
> Asher says, "I don't know. I can't."
>
> Mr. Wiley responds, "You can. Let's think about it. They all stopped paying attention and laughed. What if someone was really behind and needed this lesson? Or what if some of them will now be off-task for the rest of the class because they were distracted after seeing a pencil being thrown? What about how your classmates would

have felt if they were hit with a pencil? Wow, that would not have been a good thing."

Asher replies, "I can't fix what I did. It's over."

"I understand where you are coming from," Mr. Wiley reassures him. "But we can repair this. What are a couple of ways that you could speak to everyone in the class at the same time?"

After a moment of thinking, Asher suggests, "I can talk to them as a group."

Smiling, Mr. Wiley replies, "Wow, see, I knew you got this. So let's talk to them all at once. Now let's practice what you're going to say."

This was a tough one, but it is a typical discussion. It would be easier to just say, "Asher, you need to apologize to the entire class." But for true learning to occur and for behavior to change long-term, you want this to come from the student, with your guidance. Once you practice this a few times, it will become easier.

The trepidation of going in front of peers and apologizing is impactful. Have the students practice and role-play what they will say a few times, first, and set firm expectations. "Thank you for practicing what you're going to say and for taking responsibility for how your action impacted others. After this is done, that part of the consequence is completely over. If you go up there and don't take this seriously, though, understand that I will have to give you a bigger consequence." You don't have to let them know what this will be, but preview that it will come. We've done this for over ten years, and have only had a handful of students fail to take it seriously.

If you have led them through this process successfully, they will buy into the success of the apology.

Next, the students must repair the harm with the other student or students. See Hack 1 (Let's Talk) and Hack 2 (Circle Up) for more information on those mediations.

Regardless of whether you end with your one-on-one conversation or move on to circling up, the final product should be an action item to repair the harm, which will allow all stakeholders to move on. Some examples are letters of apology, face-to-face apologies, community service, creating a lesson around the negatives of a behavior ("Why using curse words in school/work won't lead to success") and presenting it, writing a report that relates to their displayed behavior, and/or having the student facilitate a peer group around a behavior they chose (run an anti-bullying lesson). The sky is the limit with this. Just remember that it must be logical and related to the behavior.

STEP 4: Reintegrate.

Once students have repaired the harm with all stakeholders, it is time for them to reintegrate into the classroom. This is also the time for resetting the room. Example: "I know we just had a little bit of a distraction, but Asher did a great job of apologizing. So let's jump back into where we left off. Before we start, though, remember that we are all in this together. I'm proud of you. Now where was I …"

This is a quick and easy way to pull everyone back in as a community. Try to do a check-in with Asher later, as well. Example: "Hey, you did great up there earlier with the apology and squashing the situation with Finlee. This is the way I like to see you. Keep it going!" End it with a good high-five and a smile. The rule of thumb is that for every redirection, there should be three affirmations—ideally on the same day. Remember, relationships are everything.

OVERCOMING PUSHBACK

Let me preface this section with the statement that data talks. You can quickly find overwhelming trends in data showing that restorative practices work. It's worth it. We've practiced this for over ten years now and have found it to be advantageous for all parties. That doesn't mean everyone will agree.

THIS WON'T WORK FOR ALL STUDENTS. Sure, it might not be effective for all students at all times in all situations. Students are unique, and so are the specific circumstances that led to the conflict. Students have different backgrounds, levels of support at home, and levels of adverse childhood experiences. I can tell you that the current punitive system doesn't have a one-size-fits-all working model. I can also tell you that restorative discipline develops empathy at an exponential rate, strengthens relationships, and cultivates positive communication—even if it isn't 100-percent effective. Restorative discipline might not be a silver bullet, but it is a highly effective tool for your toolbox, and it has a better chance of reaching all the individual characters than a punitive system does.

IT IS TOO COMPLICATED. We get it; sending a student to the office is way easier. But we're not telling you any secrets when we say it doesn't work. That behavior will continue as soon as that student returns, and it might even get worse. It also drastically affects the climate of your classroom when a student is sent out and returns without repairing anything. Once you start using restorative discipline, you won't go back. These practices do not mean that you can never send a student to the office with a referral, because you will still have to in some circumstances. Even when this is the case, restorative discipline still has its place, as the student can repair the harm before reintegrating into the classroom. This is what restores the classroom climate.

ALL TEACHERS AREN'T TRAINED. There are several options out there for this. Recommend this book to them, or allow them to shadow you while you have a conversation and mediation. Once teachers see this in action, they become advocates. We have seen these practices grow like wildfire when fellow teachers see the results.

Put simply, restorative justice addresses the growing crisis in our schools around discipline. The school-to-prison pipeline is real, and alarming. With restorative discipline, however, we can stop that trend.

CAN'T TEACH AN OLD DOG NEW TRICKS. Change is hard. If you're a seasoned teacher, why change? Teaching isn't just math, science, and English anymore; it's everything. Students need us to teach them how to be successful. They need to learn the skills necessary for resolving conflict, using their voices, and making things right when they stumble. A ticket to the principal's office won't do any of that, but sitting down with them to discuss their actions and teach them how to improve will.

THE HACK IN ACTION

I'm on monitoring lunch duty, the best of all duties, and I notice a commotion coming from the back table. When I make it through the crowd of students and cell phones, I see James, with tears in his eyes, being pulled by one of his friends toward the exit. I also notice Craig pacing back and forth, covered in milk. What a great day to be on lunch duty.

I radio for assistance, and move to keep both students separated while I decide what should happen next. These two are always together and are friends, so this is odd. Since he was the more agitated of the two (and thus more potentially volatile), I go to talk with James. He walks me through how Craig kept talking about how James was fat and that was why no one wanted to go to Homecoming with him. James said, "We all laughed the first time, since he gives me a hard time about my weight a lot. I just wasn't feeling it after the sixteenth time, ya know? So I slapped his milk out of his mouth." He then says that Craig pushed past the table and started trying to hit him until someone else pulled him back.

James is able to identify what he did wrong and how he was feeling at the time. James also agrees to have a mediation with Craig to squash the situation and tell him how he felt about their interactions leading up to and including the conflict in the cafeteria. When I discuss the situation with Craig, his story matches up, and he also admits that what he did was wrong.

We go into the open classroom at the end of the hall, away from curious passersby, and start the mediation. I open by saying, "This is about what happened in the cafeteria a few minutes ago. This was completely unacceptable behavior, but you both have agreed to fix what happened with this mediation. Do you both agree that we can resolve what happened right here and right now?"

When they nod, I continue. "Now, here are the rules. One person talks at a time. If you have a question, raise your hand. I am in charge of this mediation. If you get upset, you can walk out to cool down. If you sit right outside the door and come back in within two minutes, we will continue. If not, we will have to let this situation be handled by the dean, and he will not be open to your input. Do you both understand and agree to these norms?"

When they nod, I give the okay to get started.

I start by asking James to go over his version of what happened. James explains how Craig was making fun of his weight and saying that's why he wouldn't be going to Homecoming. He states, "I normally don't care, but I wasn't feeling it today. My mom just moved out and it's been hard." James apologizes for smacking the milk out of Craig's hand and getting it all over him.

Craig then states his side and says, "I didn't know about your mom, I'm sorry, man. I didn't mean anything by saying that stuff. You know that. I won't mess around with you about that stuff anymore."

At that point, as the mediator, I feel like the situation is resolved. So I say, "Thank you, guys. You both did great. Do you both feel like this situation is squashed?" They nod, and I say, "I agree; I think this situation is squashed. Now for the next part of the consequence. You both caused a huge scene in the cafeteria, and you made a mess. After school today, you will both stay after and sweep, mop, and clean the entire cafeteria. I will let the janitor know and set it up. Meet in the cafeteria at 3:45. Once this is done, this situation will be over."

PRO TIP: Additional stakeholders (students who sat around the table, parents, and students who might have contributed to the issue) can be invited into the mediation. This can be utilized when other students were involved in the issue, or when you're dealing with a tough student who will benefit from hearing from peers.

Restorative discipline takes incidents that might otherwise result in punishment and instead recognizes the opportunity. Conflicts are opportunities for students to understand the impact of their behavior, understand their obligation to take responsibility for their actions, and take steps toward making things right. Allowing them to work through the problem and develop their own ways to repair the harm sets the foundation to change their behaviors permanently, rather than just putting a Band-Aid on a single situation.

HACK 4

THROW OUT THE RULES
CREATE CLEAR AND CONSISTENT EXPECTATIONS

The expectations that others play on us help
us form our expectations of ourselves.
—WES MOORE, CEO OF ROBIN HOOD AND AUTHOR OF
THE OTHER WES MOORE: ONE NAME, TWO FATES

THE PROBLEM: RELYING ON RULES DOESN'T WORK

THE CLASSROOM SHOULD be a place where students feel at home. For some, this replicates the sense of safety and belonging they have in their own homes, while for others, the classroom provides a safe refuge from the stress and instability of their personal lives. We often get so caught up in test scores, differentiation of instruction, and daily classroom behaviors—those tried and true rules—that we forget to be vigilant about building a positive culture in our classrooms. Classroom culture does not just happen; it is built, nurtured, and sustained.

It is not the right rules that make a classroom a great place for students to be; it is the right relationships and expectations.

What's the problem with rules? First, they often focus on specific behaviors that we want to prevent, while failing to address the bigger picture. For example, one teacher might have a rule that students cannot throw paper. Unfailingly, she will have that one student who throws a highlighter across the room and claims that punishment would be unfair because he didn't technically break the rule (it wasn't paper, after all). Children are experts at finding loopholes. Rules that are too specific tempt the most innovative and mischievous students to challenge the boundaries.

Second, rules typically only teach students how *not* to behave, and often only apply to specific circumstances. Take gum-chewing, for example. Is it ever appropriate for kids to chew gum? Yes. So do we really want to teach students not to chew gum at all? Or is our goal to teach them to chew it without disturbing others (be respectful) and to dispose of it properly when they're finished (maintain a safe and clean environment)? There is something to be said for teaching students to follow the spirit of the law and not just the letter of the law. There will never be a specific rule that applies in every instance, or for everything you might encounter as a teacher. We have to learn to think outside of the box—and around the rules.

THE HACK: THROW OUT THE RULES

If students knew how to be successful independently, they would do it. But students need to be taught what to do, and that goes above and beyond teaching them what *not* to do. Teachers must expect success but also equip students with the tools necessary to reach our high expectations.

This starts with setting expectations that we hold students to, students hold each other to, and students hold themselves to. It's important to think of these points as expectations rather than rules. And teachers may find that they have even more freedom with these broad expectations. They'll allow you to run the kind of classroom environment you believe is best for students, and give you the flexibility to adjust to new and unique situations.

Start by listing your ideal set of classroom norms, and then posting them in a place where students can see them. Make sure they're clear and easy for students to understand, and that they know how vital these expectations are to your classroom and to their learning experience. We cannot expect students to adhere to the expectations if they are not aware of their importance.

From here, the norms become your foundation for guiding students toward positive behaviors.

Imagine your students are supposed to be conducting online research. You circulate around the room, ready to answer questions and provide guidance, and come across a student who is playing a racing game instead of researching the Amazon Rainforest. He looks up, realizes he's busted, and quickly tries to switch tabs. Your conversation could go something like this:

"Hey, Juan. I see you're researching birds that live in the Amazon Rainforest. That's a pretty broad topic. I bet if you narrowed your search down to a specific kind of bird, you'd find better resources. That will make it easier to engage in productive work. Is there any particular bird that interests you thus far?" (Pause to give him a chance to answer.) "No? Okay, I'll be back around in a few minutes to see if you need additional help narrowing your search. Let me know how it goes!"

In this scenario, you did not have to allude to a specific rule, nor did you direct the student away from the negative behavior. Instead, you provided him with the coaching he needed to move toward the desired behavior. You reminded him of the expectation (engage in productive work) by giving him the nudge he needed to do so successfully (narrowing his search). Hopefully, this guidance and your reappearance in a few minutes will keep Juan on-task and away from gaming.

> INVOLVING STUDENTS IN CREATING THE EXPECTATIONS ALLOWS CLASS-WIDE CONVERSATIONS ABOUT HOW THE EXPECTATIONS, AND BREAKING THEM, AFFECT ALL THE STUDENTS.

Be mindful of the goal for all students to be held to the same expectations. If you expect all students to engage in productive work, then you must hold all students accountable. Perhaps you felt the need to redirect Juan because you know he struggles in your class. A while later, you notice another student, Jeremy, also playing games instead of researching. Unlike Juan, Jeremy is a conscientious student, and you know that if Jeremy doesn't do his work in class, he's certain to finish it during study hall or at home. So, do you let Jeremy continue to play games? If you do, what message is that sending to the rest of the class? The expectations are in place for everyone. Just like Juan, Jeremy needs to close out the game and get back to work.

What kind of environment do you believe students need in order to be successful? What kind of classroom culture supports that environment? What attitudes, values, and habits create that culture? Let these questions be your North Star as you work to replace classroom rules with classroom expectations.

WHAT YOU CAN DO TOMORROW

Perhaps there's no better way to be restorative in your classroom than to have students develop their own rules, which builds a sense of ownership, empathy, and responsibility. Involving students in creating the expectations also allows class-wide conversations about how the expectations, and breaking them, affect all the students. Those conversations help bake empathy into the very core of how the classroom runs. To get started with building this foundation, try a few steps tomorrow, and refine your process from there.

- **HAVE A CLASS MEETING.** Have students circle up, and elect a scribe. Invite students to spend two minutes chatting with a neighbor about their favorite class or teacher, from any grade level. Ask them to focus on a classroom where they felt safe and respected and where the environment was conducive to learning. How would the student describe the teacher? Their interactions with students? Students' interactions with one another? Circulate or ask for volunteers and have the scribe record the characteristics of an ideal classroom. Next, ask students to turn and talk about the opposite sort of teacher. What conflicts have they had with teachers? What behaviors did they observe in their peers that created an environment that was hostile or did not set them up for success? Again, ask students to share and the scribe to record the answers.

- **TAKE A STEP BACK.** Next, invite students to look at the lists holistically. Chances are, they're going to notice that their favorite classrooms were supported by a culture of clear expectations, not a running list of rules. Using their list, ask the students to help you write your own classroom expectations. Yes, this process is slower and more labor-intensive than simply establishing the expectations yourself. But guiding the students' hands in crafting those same expectations means they will be just as committed to them as you are.

- **KEEP IT SHORT.** Since you're reading this book, that means it's important for you to create a classroom where everyone is respected. What behaviors would get in the way of this? Can you think of five? Fifteen? More? Probably. In fact, it would be nearly impossible to create a list of rules so exhaustive that you cover every potential problem. The classroom expectation, though, could be as simple as respecting yourself, others, and property. Short and sweet. When a student does something to disrespect a classmate, redirect that specific behavior with clear guidelines for a more appropriate, respectful alternative.

Maybe disorder is your pet peeve. Perhaps gum on the bottoms of desks, ruffles left behind from perforated paper, and candy wrappers are like nails on a chalkboard. You find yourself compulsively pushing in chairs and returning supplies to their bins throughout the day. Worse yet is trying to navigate the narrow spaces between desks when students' bookbags and coats litter the walkways. It would feel like you needed a laundry list of rules to maintain order. No chewing gum. Throw away all trash. No candy. Push in your chairs. Return supplies. Keep bookbags and coats under your desk ... whew! Does that cover it? Wait ... last week, someone in third period spilled juice on a desk and didn't clean it up, leaving a sticky mess for you to find later. Better add a ban on juice, or maybe even all drinks, just to be safe.

Maybe not. Instead, how about one simple expectation that covers all of these problems plus anything else that would lead to disorder? The answer: Maintain a safe and clean environment.

A BLUEPRINT FOR FULL IMPLEMENTATION

Throwing out the rules will require a consistent commitment to rethinking your approach to addressing student behaviors. Students will need to understand the expectations and be held accountable to them. Here are three main ways that you can help ensure that expectations will work in your classroom:

STEP 1: Rethink redirection.

We want to focus on guiding students toward the kinds of decisions that will lead to their success, so it's important that we acknowledge and validate these behaviors when we see them.

Sometimes, the best redirection is actually no direction at all. The students have just finished painting, and it's time to clean up and get ready for math review. Cory decides he doesn't want to clean up or do math and throws himself on the ground in a tantrum. You decide to ignore him, and instead, help the other students put away the supplies and thank them for their cooperation. Realizing his tantrum isn't getting him what he wants, Cory gets up and sits down for his math lesson. Now is the time for you to notice him. Smile and thank him for his help. The students who are being responsible and following directions will learn that their actions are desirable and help the classroom environment to be successful, while the students who are not being responsible will quickly realize that their actions do not add value to the success of the classroom.

Teenage students may not throw a full-blown tantrum, but their defiance can still disrupt a classroom. For adolescents, focusing on the behaviors you are looking for early in the year should help set the tone for the other school days. Learners at this grade level tend to notice what behaviors are rewarded and recognized. If a student acts out or loudly interrupts learning, continue to focus positive attention on the students who are engaged in the lesson and who are acting respectfully toward the teacher and their peers. If the student continues to act out, check out Step 3.

Additionally, giving students voice and choice is a great way to reinforce positive behavior. When a student has shown diligence and responsibility by completing his work on time, consider offering him two or three choices for the next activity. Being able to choose how to spend his time reinforces his positive behavior and models for his peers that responsibility can lead to certain freedoms.

STEP 2: Establish restorative justice.

As important as it is for students to know what you expect of them, they also need to know what will happen if those expectations aren't met. Ideally, your school will have a behavior system in place that outlines restorative strategies (more to come on that later), provides a way to document behaviors across all classes, and addresses recidivism. If this isn't the case, you'll need to create your own system. Through the help of this book, you or your school will be able to implement practices that are truly restorative for students. For now, whether you use a demerit system, a behavior chart, or something else, you need to establish consequences if you have not done so already. Setting and communicating consequences early allows you to address the student calmly and prevents a power struggle. The student already understands the result; it isn't personal when you're simply following through on something you established from the beginning.

STEP 3: Preview, warn, and give consequences.

Having expectations instead of rules does not mean you never address specific behaviors. Use the following steps to keep the class in line in terms of behavior.

- **PREVIEW.** The preview is the whole-group reminder of your expectations, and this can include more specific guidance so students know how to meet the expectation. The preview can also address anticipated pain points. For example, students are getting started on a jigsaw reading activity. As they settle into their seats, you remind them of the expectation: Engage in productive work. Explain how that should look.

  "You have fifteen minutes to read and summarize your section of the article. You should be engaged in productive work the whole time. Please leave your cell phones in your pockets or bags so you're not distracted. If you finish before the fifteen minutes are up, use that time to start tonight's reading on Page 107."

  Now students know exactly what to do to be successful. They know they need to engage in productive work, they know that this means keeping their cell phones put away (your anticipated pain point), and they know how to use extra time if they finish early.

- **WARN.** A warning addresses one student or group of students, not the whole class. The warning should be a reminder of the expectation, should address the behavior that does not meet the expectation, and should preview the consequence that will be given if the unwanted behavior continues.

Let's go back to the example above. Students are working on the jigsaw reading, and you see Ayanna has her head down. You kneel next to her and, leading with empathy, ask what's up. (Remember to address the person before the problem.) "I'm done," she tells you. "Awesome. Thanks for finishing the summary. Having your head down isn't productive, though. Please start on tonight's reading on Page 107. It would disappoint me to have to record this incident or contact home after you've written such a thorough summary."

You've reminded Ayanna of your expectation to engage in productive work, addressed the unwanted behavior of putting her head down, and previewed the consequence of behavior points if the unwanted behavior continues. At this point, you should smile and give Ayanna some space to comply. Give her a minute to come around as you circulate. If she does, reinforce the positive behavior with a smile, thumbs-up, or "thank you" the next time you pass by.

- **GIVE CONSEQUENCES.** Previewing and warning only work to enforce the norms if you follow through with consequences when necessary. The consequences should be as understood as the expectations. The students should know exactly what will happen if they choose to continue a behavior after the warning, and then you need to know exactly how you will follow through. Only give one warning. If you give more than one warning to a student, the other students will expect multiple warnings as well, and this can lead to power struggles. When assigning consequences, coach students through the behavior so they understand the harm that they have caused to others, and are given a chance to repair the harm.

Maintaining relationships with students and maintaining the culture by enforcing the norms can feel like a tricky balance, but the more you front-load, the less personal redirection you have to do. Maybe Ayanna is one of your favorite students, but it took weeks for her to warm up to you. You see that she has gotten out her book and opened it to Page 107, but her head is down next to the book. You really don't want to endanger the rapport you've only recently developed. Should you give her another warning? No. You only give one warning, or your warnings mean nothing.

Approach Ayanna, kneel next to her again, and give the consequence. "Ayanna, I'm disappointed to see your head down again. I know it can be hard to stay focused, but we've talked about active reading strategies to engage your mind. Unfortunately, I'm going to have to record this incident for not following our class norms. I really don't like doing this, so I hope when we move into the next part of the activity, I will see you engaged in discussion the whole time. You're a smart kid; let's not rack up consequences for silly behaviors."

By giving the consequence, you're ensuring that your classroom will remain a place where students can expect to work hard. By empathizing with Ayanna, you're showing her that the consequence isn't personal.

Remember that enforcing the norms isn't about not liking the students; it's a necessary part of maintaining a classroom culture where all students are held accountable. Having established consequences makes redirection business, not personal. It's important to be vigilant about giving consequences equitably. The kind of relationship you have with a student should play no part in how you hold that student accountable. The expectations and consequences must be the same for everyone. The only exception should be students who have exceptional needs, and you should work closely with your student support services team to plan a specific course of action appropriate for these students.

OVERCOMING PUSHBACK

Students, parents, and administrators are used to teachers providing a list of ten or more rules that address specific behaviors. It might make them feel uneasy to receive what they could interpret as a generic, vague list of expectations.

KIDS NEED RULES FOR EVERYTHING. Explain that you are guiding students toward the behaviors you want to see. For example, students can maintain a safe and clean environment in a number of ways. You want to reinforce the positive habits that foster that expectation. Students can then carry these habits forward to become better community members. We need to stress the need for expectations over rules and for ownership of a positive learning environment instead of compliance.

MY JOB IS TO TEACH; PARENTS SHOULD WORRY ABOUT CHARACTER. Yes, parents should have instilled X, Y, and Z in their kids. Yes, parents should be supportive of their kids' education. But it's not the kids' fault if they don't have that sort of foundation. Also, kids learn from many important people in their lifetime, and their teachers are critical in this development. In fact, many students spend more time with their teachers than they do their own parents, due to parent work schedules and other circumstances.

Parents do not have to take a course in parenting or learn how to help their children succeed in school. As teachers, we must also help parents understand how they can support what we do at school through constant communication and collaboration.

If we want to alter a kid's trajectory, we must do things that are not on our curriculum map. Everything we do connects back to academics, anyway. Students need to know how to behave so that they can successfully complete their work. They need to know how to behave so that their peers can successfully complete *their* work. They learn this through the enforcement of clear expectations.

THE HACK IN ACTION

At Purdue Polytechnic High School in Indianapolis, Indiana, students might be in ten or more academic spaces throughout their day. Teachers, referred to there as coaches, do not have their own classrooms, and so they teach, monitor, and coach students in various spaces in the building. For students, knowing the rules of a certain teacher or space could be very difficult. The same room might have numerous teachers throughout the day, and therefore the rules could change as one teacher walks in and one teacher walks out. In many secondary schools, students also face different rules from numerous teachers and classrooms in a day, though often not different teachers in the same classrooms.

In some learning labs or study areas, food was allowed (much to the dismay of those teachers who did not allow food and who felt frustrated by the collection of crumbs on the floor). In other instances, cell phones were allowed to be out by some teachers but not by others. When it was time for the teachers to transition and for new teachers to enter the spaces, many students got in trouble for breaking the new teacher's rules even though they were following the rules of the teacher who had been overseeing the space only minutes before.

Inconsistencies in rules regularly caused students not only to be confused, but sometimes combative with teachers. They pointed out that another teacher allowed them to do whatever offense that they were now getting in trouble for. Of course, this also led to tension among the instructional staff, as students pitted educators against one another intentionally to avoid being "in trouble."

Realizing that teachers had their own rules, and the list of permissible behaviors within any given learning space was ever-changing, administrators identified that the problem was not only inconsistencies for students, but also that rules were not the answer at all. Instead, they needed clear, schoolwide expectations. The administrators collected many of the teachers' rules and made a few short umbrella expectations that focused on what students should be doing instead of listing out the numerous things that they should *not* be doing.

Instead of:

- Cell phones are not allowed (depending on the teacher).

- Food is not allowed (depending on the teacher).

- Maintain a whisper-voice when done with assignments (depending on the teacher).

The expectations became:

- Engage in productive work.

- Maintain a safe and clean environment.

- Share space effectively.

Signs were added in every learning space, and the teachers and staff at the school received training on how to uphold the expectations as a united front. For example, when a class or learning experience began, teachers were encouraged to preview the expectations with students to reestablish and reinforce the expectations. When a student was off-task, the teachers were coached to refer to the specific expectation that was not being met.

For example, instead of saying "Get off that game" or "Stop talking to your neighbor," a teacher might say, "Please refer to expectation one, which is to engage in productive work." Once teachers collectively addressed the norms, and the students heard the same message everywhere in the building regardless of which teacher was supervising, students began to see that they were expected to uphold the norms throughout the building and could not look for differences in the spaces or instructors.

Instead of focusing on telling students what we don't want them to do, we should help them understand how to make choices that will lead to positive lifelong habits. Teaching students how to engage in productive work, maintain a safe and clean environment, and share the space effectively with others will hopefully teach them to become better citizens than students who are only taught not to chew gum.

We need to be consistent in how we redirect behaviors, however, and we have to be fair and equitable about assigning consequences. Maintaining our relationships with students and maintaining our expectations are not mutually exclusive; they are one and the same. Students need love, but they also need structure, safety, and predictability. In the next chapter, we will go beyond positive behavior supports, expectations, and rules, and into restorative measures that help create long-lasting changes in behaviors.

CREATE A GROWTH MINDSET
PUT STUDENTS BACK IN THE DRIVER'S SEAT

*Whether you think you can, or you
think you can't, you're right.*

—HENRY FORD, FOUNDER OF THE FORD MOTOR COMPANY

THE PROBLEM: TOO MANY STUDENTS
MAINTAIN A FIXED MINDSET

HAVE YOU EVER asked a teacher from the grade below you which students you need to keep a close eye on? Or have you been warned about a handful of students known to be troublemakers? Before these students have even walked through the doors of our classrooms, we have already labeled them as "this kind of student" or "that kind of student." Categorizing others and ourselves is a natural human tendency that helped our ancestors distinguish allies from those who presented a danger. Today, we continue to place ourselves and others in narrowly defined boxes. Some students are good at math. Some are not. Some students are hard workers. Others only cause distractions. Some students have attitude problems, just like the older siblings you struggled to teach in prior years.

When it comes to restorative circles, this becomes even more important, because those preconceived ideas make it harder for you as the teacher to accept a student's apology or commitment to change. A student who harbors these ideas about themselves can also find it difficult to believe they can do any better.

Think like a student for a second. The teacher is doing a lesson on something new and you are sitting there wondering if your classmates are as confused as you are. Of course, you assume that you are one of the only ones who doesn't get it, so you don't raise your hand because you don't want to embarrass yourself. What you don't realize, however, is that many of your classmates are feeling exactly like you: confused, overwhelmed, and a little frustrated.

When you finally try it, you fail, and you get a little upset. But then you try again and keep trying, and your perseverance and grit pay off and you learn the new skill. Soon, you're doing it like it's second nature—and no longer worrying about whether it took the other students several tries before they got it.

It probably did. Learning, in any form, works the same for everyone. As Thomas Fuller said, "All things are difficult before they are easy." Sure, some kids might have learned or grasped the skill more quickly than you did, but a secret exists about many of those who get things quickly: when they *don't* get it quickly, they give up. Many students who are considered quick learners build their identities around how naturally smart or talented they are. They are used to things coming easily, and not having to work as hard as others. The problem with this, however, is that once they face an obstacle that is not easily or quickly overcome, they do not know what to do. They get frustrated, feel bad for themselves, and sometimes give up.

Unlike students who are used to trying something multiple times, they lack the foundation to take multiple stabs at a problem.

Dr. Carol Dweck, professor of psychology at Stanford University and author of *Mindset*, describes this rigidity of thought—this inability to look at learning as a process—as a "fixed mindset." People with fixed mindsets believe traits like character, intelligence, and talent are fixed and cannot be changed. Those with a fixed mindset are especially afraid of failure and resistant to criticism, because they believe they can't do anything to improve and to ensure a better result next time. In short, they believe that they are stuck with what they've got.

Having a fixed mindset means instinctively avoiding what you are not naturally good at. For example, if you believe you are not good at math, you might think that you will be bad at math no matter what you do, and see no point in trying. In the example above, a student who did not understand what the teacher was saying right away, or who did not catch on to new strategies as quickly as his classmates, might have given up and simply considered himself a bad reader. This fixed mindset could have kept the student from wanting to read at all.

In an academic setting, a fixed mindset prevents students from embracing challenges. If students don't understand something on the first try, or after minimal effort, they decide that it's pointless to continue trying. Their intelligence, after all, is fixed, and no matter how much they try, they can't change the fact that they don't understand something. Effort is pointless. Trying certainly will only lead to failure. The students may become inundated with negative self-talk, and then fixated on ways they think they aren't good enough.

Many students go from there to masking their perceived short-comings and vulnerabilities with disruptive behaviors. A student may hope that if he goofs off during geometry, no one will realize that when the teacher asks him to calculate the area of a trapezoid, she may as well be speaking in Spanish (oh, and he's failing that, too). Instead of feeling stupid in front of everyone, he flicks the ear of the kid in front of him, so he'll be asked to step into the hallway. It doesn't matter to him if he misses the lesson, and there's no point in doing the homework the teacher is about to go over. He'll never be good at math, anyway.

And just like that, a fixed mindset and the belief that he's not good enough becomes a self-fulfilling prophecy.

Socially, a fixed mindset becomes an excuse to shirk responsibility. A student with a fixed mindset and a bad temper will resist strategies to manage her anger. Someone with a fixed mindset is likely to assign blame in a conflict rather than accepting responsibility. The person sees any problem between two people as irreparable, since character traits cannot be changed. In a restorative circle, the students may not be open to exploring ways of approaching any problems in the future, since they don't think anything can change in that regard. When presented with growth opportunities, these students might respond, "This is how I've always been, and this is how I'll always be."

A student who believes she is incapable of change is not likely to embrace restorative circles and practices. She might never reach her social, emotional, or academic potential. If students do not believe they can get better at something, it will impact all areas of their lives, limiting their current and future growth. This might ultimately lead to them not succeeding in school and life, potentially reducing their chances of graduation or finding a good job.

As teachers, we must find ways to help them outgrow that fixed mindset, and develop a growth mindset instead.

THE HACK: CREATE A GROWTH MINDSET

The first step toward helping students build a growth mindset is boosting their confidence. Many students misbehave because they don't feel successful academically. If we can build their confidence, the behavior will often take care of itself. Most kids care, even if they don't show it. If they're giving up before they start, due to a fixed mindset, they're killing their own confidence, and therefore their own success. Build those kids up and watch them grow. Students need to believe in their capacity to change and succeed before they will fully invest effort in whatever skill they're trying to master.

There are a number of ways to teach about growth vs. fixed mindsets, but connecting it to your students' own experiences will result in faster internalization. Instead of leading with the concepts of a growth or fixed mindset, which might be confusing, set students up for a reflection where they will naturally stumble upon a time when they had a growth mindset.

MANY STUDENTS MISBEHAVE BECAUSE THEY DON'T FEEL SUCCESSFUL ACADEMICALLY. IF WE CAN BUILD THEIR CONFIDENCE, THE BEHAVIOR WILL OFTEN TAKE CARE OF ITSELF.

1. Ask students to recall the first time they did something that they are now pretty good at. Common examples are riding a bike, shooting free throws, and cooking. Students can share these stories in small groups.

2. Next, have the students map out the steps they took to advance from beginner to their current level. A student might have started riding with training wheels on a flat sidewalk, then moved up to a bike with coaster brakes and taken on a steep driveway. After enough bumps and bruises, the student can now coast through the neighborhood with no hands.

3. Whatever their personal journey, have students draw out the steps it took to get them from the start to their present locations. Students can share these in small circles.

4. Explain that students just explored a time when they had a growth mindset—when they believed their abilities could be improved with practice. Use this as an example of what can happen in the classroom as well.

5. Hang some of these progressions on the walls and reference them later to reassure students that growth is possible through hard work.

Use the term "growth mindset" frequently so students internalize the idea that with enough effort, they can improve or change. As students enter restorative circles, remind them to maintain a growth mindset about themselves, their peers, and the culture of their class as a whole.

The famous phrase, "Hard work beats talent when talent doesn't work hard" by high school coach Tim Notke also applies to academics. It is when students go the extra mile, study hard, seek help, and never give up that they succeed. Instead of getting frustrated when they don't get something immediately, or get a bad grade, help them see those situations as opportunities for improvement. If they give up on something, it will only get worse with time, as they usually need to understand the lesson or concept they are currently working on to understand the next lesson or concept.

The growth mindset establishes an important environment in your classroom, and makes for resilient learners. It promotes better relationships as the students constructively challenge one another to become better versions of themselves. Students with a growth mindset are also more likely to take responsibility for their actions, because they believe in their capacity to learn and do better next time, which is a critical component of restorative discipline.

WHAT YOU CAN DO TOMORROW

Changing a whole mindset can feel like an insurmountable task, but small steps can bring big change. Students need to believe in their ability to grow and change as people before they will buy into restorative practices. Start building your plans for changing mindsets in your classroom with the following tips:

- **INTRODUCE A GROWTH MINDSET.** Invite students to bring photos of themselves as small children enjoying a meal. The first birthday cake "smash" is perfect for this activity. Ask them to display their photos (digital or print) on their desks. Walk around with a clipboard and a *good activity*

pen, nodding in approval at the photos starring neat eaters, and *tsk* disapprovingly at photos with messy eaters. After concluding your walk, announce a special dinner event being hosted by the PTO, and you've been asked to recruit a number of your students to serve as ambassadors. You don't want to be embarrassed, so you are going to choose the students who will best represent you at the dining table. List the names of the students whose photos featured clean faces as being potential selections.

Hopefully, the students will quickly point out that when they were two years old and wearing more of their spaghetti than they were eating, that doesn't mean they are messy eaters now. And there you have it: growth mindset. The vast majority of students, even those who brought photos of clean faces, started out as messy eaters, but have (hopefully) improved in the years that have followed. Their capacity for table manners was not set at birth; they had to practice and become more proficient over the years. Use this as an opportunity to discuss the growth mindset with your class.

- STRETCH OUT OF THE COMFORT ZONE. Having a growth mindset means exploring unfamiliar territory. It can be scary to learn something new, and it's much safer to stay in your comfort zone. Students need to be reassured that most people are intimidated by change and growth. Working through those feelings of discomfort is the only way to grow as a person. If we never push students out of their comfort zones, we never give them the chance to discover new passions, become resilient, and gain confidence. On the other hand, if we push students too far out of their comfort zones, or too quickly, we risk scaring them off. We must be mindful of this in our restorative practices. Keep your conferences and restorative circles reflective of the students' level of readiness, and encourage them to grow without causing them to become defensive and retreat.

The first step is to help students understand how to stretch themselves slowly but steadily. Introduce students to the idea of the Zones of Growth: Comfort Zone, Challenge Zone, and Crisis Zone. In the Comfort Zone, the student feels relaxed and in control. This is a low-stress situation. The familiarity is reassuring, and the student is confident in his or her safety and ability. A student who has played guitar for years will probably find himself in the Comfort Zone while jamming out with his friends.

In the Challenge Zone, something is uncomfortable but bearable; the student could stay in the Challenge Zone for a while, and eventually, it would become part of the Comfort Zone. Perhaps one of the friends in the jam session is working on mastering a new chord progression. He's struggling a little bit, and it feels awkward in front of his much more confident friend. The more he practices, the smoother his playing becomes. In time, his proficiency will grow, his Comfort Zone will become a little bigger, and playing that chord progression will be no big deal.

In the Crisis Zone, the student is overcome by anxiety or fear, and quickly retreats back to the Comfort Zone. In this zone, your fight/freeze/flee instincts take over. An example of this might be running from the room screaming because a spider moved two inches closer to where you are. If the Crisis Zone is significant enough, it restricts you from even thinking about expanding on it.

Once students understand these Zones of Growth, they can more readily identify the small steps they can take to move forward. Incorporate this idea into conferences and restorative circles to increase the likelihood of follow-through from your students.

- **MODEL IT.** All teachers benefit from frequently learning something they are not already familiar with or interested in. This is how students feel every day in your classroom. They are exposed to things they have never seen before and asked to do things they might not have ever done before. This is their normal, and it is tough! The best way to anticipate pain points in your students' journeys is to walk alongside them on your own parallel journey.

Before you ever introduce the students to the concept of a growth mindset, invite them to take a peek into a trip you're making through the Zones of Growth. Have you recently taken up a new hobby? Regularly display photos of your progress. Are you having a hard time mastering the newest innovation that your IT department rolled out? Let your students see you struggle through your early navigation, and celebrate in front of them when you finally figure out how to embed a video in their online assignment.

Allowing others to watch us stumble and fall puts us in a scary place of vulnerability (and too much too fast can send you straight to the Crisis Zone). If you can set aside your pride and model this vulnerability, you are sending a clear message to your class that it is safe to fail forward. Make your own incompetencies (and growing competencies) visible to your students. Doing so will establish your classroom as a safe space for students to be vulnerable—a crucial ingredient to successful restorative discipline.

A BLUEPRINT FOR FULL IMPLEMENTATION

A key factor to fostering and nurturing lasting change from a fixed mindset to a growth mindset is encouraging students to take risks without fear of failure. Students will need to get comfortable stepping out of their comfort zones, and the very foundation of how your class works, from behavior to academics, must give them many chances to succeed at that. The following steps will help you set up your class for a growth mindset culture:

STEP 1: Define the Zones of Growth.

After introducing students to the concept of Zones of Growth, help them internalize the idea through physical movement. Divide the classroom into three zones: Comfort Zone, Challenge Zone, and Crisis Zone. Have all students gather in the Comfort Zone. Present scenarios and ask them to move into the Challenge Zone or Crisis Zone as they see fit. Start simple: Present students with a scenario like public speaking. Ask students to stand in the zone that represents how they would feel if asked to give a speech to the class. Once students have moved, ask for volunteers from each section to explain why they chose that zone. Move students through a few more scenarios, have them share each time, and then invite them back to their seats.

As a class, examine each scenario one at a time. What could a student in the Crisis Zone do to become more comfortable there? What smaller steps could a student in the Challenge Zone do to move toward being comfortable without moving so quickly that it pushes him into the Crisis Zone?

Ask students to devise their own scenarios. What is something they would love to do if they weren't afraid? What small steps could they take to expand their Comfort Zone into the Challenge Zone? What should they avoid doing to stay out of the Crisis Zone?

Every time you introduce a new skill or concept, ask students where they would place it on their Zones of Growth. For example, a student who is not a fan of reading might put the *Romeo and Juliet* unit in the Crisis Zone, while her neighbor, who had the starring role in last year's school play, might easily consider this a Comfort Zone unit. Discuss, as a class, steps students can take to move backward from Crisis to Challenge. An example of this is reading a modernized version or summary of a scene online before reading it aloud in class. Similarly, explore ways for students in the Comfort Zone to stretch themselves, maybe memorizing sections and performing them in front of the class.

Students need to believe in their own capacity to grow and change. When they successfully grow in the classroom, it gives them more confidence to engage in personal growth. This is crucial to restorative practices, especially a restorative circle and a re-entry circle. Identifying opportunities for growth and breaking those opportunities into manageable steps will propel students into the Challenge Zone, where real change can occur.

STEP 2: Become aware of your own comfort zone.

It is just as important for you as it is for the students to start each day and enter each restorative circle with a growth mindset. Asking students to reflect honestly on their choices and take responsibility for their actions puts them in a vulnerable place (potentially a Crisis Zone), and you need to set yourself up as the students' teammate, someone who believes they can make better choices.

Start by letting go of preconceived notions you bring to the table by intentionally looking for positives. We suggest choosing one student for observation, and particularly a student with whom you've had negative encounters in the past. Watch that student and take note of positive traits that you missed before. Opening yourself back up to a student who has been disrespectful in the past might make your heart pound (Crisis Zone alert!). Just like the way you're teaching your students, start small. Choose a step that is challenging but not impossible, like writing positive notes on that student's work or making sure to individually wish that student a good day. Once your Comfort Zone expands, move on to the next step, which might be inviting that student to eat lunch in your classroom or calling home to report positive behavior.

STEP 3: Reevaluate your grading practices.

Unfortunately, many of us are talking the talk, but not walking the walk when it comes to growth mindset in the learning process—especially in grading practices.

Grades, whether we like them or not, are one of the biggest factors in college acceptance. Failing grades are one of the biggest risk factors in students dropping out. Wouldn't it make sense to ensure that students can demonstrate growth and learn from mistakes in our classes? Many traditional grading practices reward students for being good at school—either in behavior or natural ability. In fact, many students see grades as an accumulation of points they need to obtain instead of a demonstration of mastery.

This isn't healthy, and the change starts in the classroom. Here are four grading practices that can kill a growth mindset:

- TAKING POINTS OFF FOR LATE WORK. This is punitive and inaccurately reflects achievement. Did the student know 80 percent of the material, yet get a 50 percent on the assignment? If so, the student's grade is a reflection of behavior rather than achievement. Worse yet is not taking late work at all, which demoralizes students because they have no chance to recover from a mistake. Mathematically, zeros are almost impossible to overcome.

- NOT ALLOWING RETAKES ON ASSIGNMENTS OR ASSESSMENTS. If students are supposed to learn from mistakes, wouldn't it make sense to give them a redo? Does it make sense that students can retake entire courses, yet not an assessment in our classrooms? We must decide if it is more important for students to know material on a certain day, or for them to keep going until they get it. What are we saying if students got a failing grade on something, and have no chance to fix it? If students failed an assignment, it is likely that they will fail that same concept on the quiz, test, and final. It is a snowball effect that could be prevented early on.

- ALLOWING RETAKES, BUT AVERAGING THE ATTEMPTS. Most major tests, including the ACT, SAT, driver's license test, pilot's license test, and the Bar Exam, allow the people taking them to do so as many times as they want and keep the highest scores. By averaging attempts in a class at school, we are reporting on both what the student used to and currently knows, instead of just current mastery.

- **GRADING HOMEWORK/CLASSWORK FOR ACCURACY ON A FIRST ATTEMPT.** Most students have a hard time when they do something the first time. What if we were only allowed to ride a bike once and got assessed on it? Free your students to try new concepts in a low-pressure setting. Moving to graded assessment right away makes students anxious; either they give up right away when they can't work through problems without direct teacher help, or they cheat. Many students must be exposed to concepts several times before mastering them. Try to avoid grading initial work, or make it worth very little of the overall term grade. (For more on reevaluating grading practices, see the book *Hacking Classroom Management*, Hack 7: Reassess How You Assess.)

STEP 4: Teach students how to plan and study.

A helpful way to keep students motivated, and keep them from having to overcome obstacles as often, is to be better prepared in the first place. Students' lives are hectic with homework, house chores, sports, activities, and more. They need to keep a calendar (or use an online one) with all of their responsibilities, and plan out when they will study or do homework. Also, encourage them to schedule time to relax and have a little fun.

Successful students study smartly, too. Cramming for a test is a stressful and ineffective way to prepare. Instead, encourage them to study each subject for at least a few minutes every night. This way, they will be able to identify weaknesses in their comprehension in advance of the test, which gives them enough time to go to their teachers or others who can help them. It is also important to actually study in an effective way. One of the best ways to study is to take the material they are learning and create their own test questions. By doing this, they are identifying the most important information, and also banking the information in their memory.

PRO TIP: Some students might want the path of least resistance, only doing what is comfortable. They might prefer teachers who are easy on them and who have low expectations. Later, these students will wish they had teachers who pushed them and held them to high expectations. The concept of high expectations does not mean no mistakes, no second chances, or moving fast. It means:

- Doing challenging things
- Doing challenging things until getting them right
- Working hard
- Asking for help

OVERCOMING PUSHBACK

Asking students to risk the vulnerability that comes with failure is no small feat. Set them up for early successes that will make an immediate impact. Your students need to believe that your investment is sincere.

THIS WON'T HELP MY GRADE RIGHT NOW. Students who have struggled might only be interested in investing in work guaranteed to immediately improve their grades. Show them how a growth mindset will help both their short-term and long-term success. You can get student buy-in a number of ways, but many of them depend on your school's policies.

One idea is to offer a Growth Grade Replacement. Allow students to choose one skill they didn't master. Have them map out a plan to push into the Challenge Zone to learn this material. Then offer them the opportunity to replace the old grade upon completing a new assessment. This can be done in small circles or in conferences.

Our students love video games because they can fail over and over again without consequences. They get an immense sense of joy and accomplishment when they try numerous times and finally beat the harder levels. Growth mindset in the classroom cannot exist unless we give students those numerous opportunities to demonstrate success. If students know that they always can better themselves and have a chance in our classes, their attitude toward grades and long-term investments will be a lot more positive.

YOU'RE JUST SAYING THIS SO WE DON'T FEEL DUMB. Holding on to that old fixed mindset, students might be reluctant to believe you're genuine when you express belief in their potential. It's helpful here to provide examples of your own journey from novice to mastery, maybe with an academic or life skill. You can also go back to the tried-and-true, real-life examples of celebrities, athletes, and scientists who earned criticism as children or early professionals but went on to become the greatest in their fields.

If you can, pull an example from the student's own life. Maybe you've noticed incredible growth in the student's ability to complete multiplication problems quickly. You might go so far as to contact the student's parents, explain what you are hoping to accomplish, and ask the parent for an example of a time the student showed incredible growth.

THE HACK IN ACTION

Amarra was known for her "extra" personality, and her voice often preceded her entrance into the classroom. No one ever had to wonder what kind of mood she was in, because her facial expression, tone, and word choice left no room for interpretation. More often than not, her entrance served as a warning that it had been a long day, she was tired of the latest girl drama (though in the middle of it herself), and she had no patience left for immature boys.

Most days, her teachers were an opposing army. Her attitude became her armor and her weapons, and she was not afraid to direct her daggers right at the hearts of anyone who could be a threat. Contacting her mother left little doubt about where Amarra learned her attitude, so the teachers were on their own. Restorative circles never quite made the lasting difference for which the teachers had hoped, because Amarra simply couldn't buy into them.

At the end of her freshman year, Amarra was invited (voluntold) to join a female leadership group that would serve as mentors for the next year's incoming freshmen. Most students stood aghast when they saw Amarra's name on the list. Really? Hadn't she cursed out the lunch lady two weeks ago? Nevertheless, she joined the ranks of the other twelve young ladies, and three times a week they participated in leadership development. Each young woman was charged with a special quality to model for their mentees, and any time a new student's success was impeded by a lack of development of that skill, the new student would be paired with the mentor specialist. Amarra's area of expertise? Anger management.

Even Amarra herself scoffed when she saw that qualifier next to her name. Like so many strong-willed students, though, she was determined to prove she could control her temper, if only to prove the other leadership girls wrong. Of course, it started as an uphill battle.

"This is how my mama is, this is how my sister is, and this is how I will always be," she declared in those moments when the fear of falling short loomed ahead.

Instead of arguing with her that she was capable of change, her teachers provided opportunities for Amarra to witness her own growth in non-threatening situations. For example, each member of the leadership team was tasked with mastering one Minute-to-Win-It game. Amarra was assigned the classic "cookie on your face" game, and she failed miserably the first half-dozen times. By the end of her third practice session, though, she could wiggle that cookie from her forehead to her mouth in forty-two seconds. Though not something she would likely list on her resume, mastering that skill did help build her confidence in her own capacity to learn.

For six weeks, Amarra worked with the other young ladies and two mentor teachers, exploring strategies to hone each of their unique skills. She learned about the biology that triggered her outbursts and how simple things like deep breathing could help her regain control. At first, the best she could do was take one deep breath before flying off the handle anyway. A couple more weeks of practice, however, and Amarra could take three deep breaths and express her anger loudly, but without the confetti of expletives.

By the time she finished the six-week program, Amarra was able to remove herself from most situations before getting herself into trouble.

Her teachers noticed a drop in the number of referrals she received each week, and at the end of the year, Amarra celebrated the first two-week stretch of referral-free schooling she'd had since she was in sixth grade. In her sophomore year, she served on the leadership team and was asked to take an active role in peer-led mediation.

None of the strategies Amarra's teachers had to offer would have made a difference if they didn't first instill in her the belief that she could change. Setting Amarra up for success in simple tasks built her confidence. Presenting the leadership group with a challenge that they were all doomed to fail at first, but that would incite riotous laughter anyway, established the leadership team as an environment where it was safe to try, fail, and grow.

Restorative discipline is rooted in the belief that involving all stakeholders in the healing process can lead to transformation among people, relationships, and communities. Before lasting transformation can occur, the person who committed the transgression must believe in one's own ability to be transformed. This starts with helping students let go of the preconceived idea that how they have been defined by others and by themselves in the past determines their limits and potential.

HACK 6

TEACH MINDFULNESS
EMPOWER STUDENTS TO RECOGNIZE AND MANAGE THEIR EMOTIONS

Challenging behavior occurs when the demands and expectations being placed upon a child outstrip the skills he has to respond adaptively.
—Ross W. Greene, author of Lost at School: Why Our Kids with Behavioral Challenges Are Falling Through the Cracks and How We Can Help Them

THE PROBLEM: STUDENTS LACK SELF-AWARENESS AND REGULATION

"Y OU NEED A serious attitude adjustment."

"Why on earth would you do that?"

"Get the chip off your shoulder."

Wouldn't it be nice if it were really that easy? Asking our students to perform a 180-degree turn in their attitude usually isn't the silver bullet we are hoping for when their seemingly irrational emotions outgrow our patience. But most of us have caught some variation of those words escaping our mouths in a moment of frustration. We should strive to remember that it's as unpleasant and inconvenient for them as those emotions are for us.

One reason students lack self-awareness and regulation is that no one has taught them how to effectively communicate what they're feeling. Sometimes, a student finds it hard to explain how he feels because he simply lacks the prior experience to identify it, or the language to label it. This might be the first time the student has had to navigate a situation, like feeling resentful of a new sibling because of how much time she requires of their parents. Students who come from homes where feelings are not openly discussed, especially if talking about feelings is actively discouraged, will also struggle.

Also, the pressure students (especially males) feel to mask any emotion that could make them seem weak or vulnerable complicates things. Not understanding a new feeling, lacking the language to talk about it, or not feeling safe to discuss and explore emotions can compound the student's already heightened emotional state to the point of losing control and presenting a challenge to the safe, respectful environment of a restorative school.

Outbursts and attitudes are rarely manipulative schemes, but rather symptoms of a skill or development gap. Adolescent brains continue to develop throughout puberty and into early adulthood, and the last part to be remodeled is the prefrontal cortex: the center for impulse control and the ability to anticipate consequences. This leaves young people reliant upon the parts of the brain associated with emotions and impulses. Because they have not mastered self-awareness and regulation, students often react before their logic has a chance to catch up with their emotions. That is, they react instead of responding, and in doing so, make choices that necessitate a conference or a restorative circle. In short, they act out because they don't know *how* to act, and cause a disruption to the class—which is what got us all here in the first place.

What's the difference between reacting and responding? Reactions are born from the immediate emotions created by the situation. When those emotions are negative, reactions can be especially damaging because they are quick, poorly planned, and sporadic. Reactions represent the feelings we have in that moment, but not necessarily who we are as people or what we value, yet their impact can be lasting. Responses, on the other hand, are tempered. We probably still feel the spur of the reaction, but staying in control and allowing that knee-jerk instinct to pass allows our logical thinking to reboot. This can save us from the regret of a word spoken in anger or a fist swung before a breath was inhaled.

> STUDENTS LEARN SELF-REGULATION BEST WHEN THEY FEEL CONNECTED AND SAFE, AND THEY FEEL CONNECTED AND SAFE WHEN EDUCATORS FOCUS ON BUILDING EMPATHY INSTEAD OF DOLING OUT PUNISHMENT.

Working with students in this crucial phase of growth means we have the opportunity to teach them the difference between the two, just as we support their writing and calculating skills. Students who can articulate and manage their emotions are more empathetic classroom community members.

THE HACK: TEACH MINDFULNESS

Mindfulness is the practice of bringing one's attention to the present moment, and promotes calm acknowledgment of one's thoughts, feelings, and physical sensations. Students who practice mindfulness are more tuned in to their emotional states and the experiences that most influence them. Restorative discipline and mindfulness go hand-in-hand. Students learn self-regulation best when they feel connected and safe, and they feel connected and safe when educators focus on building empathy instead of doling out punishment.

We can meet students where they are and build upon their current social-emotional knowledge and regulation capacity in a number of ways. Depending on the age of your students, you might start intentionally incorporating emotion-based language into the daily routine. The next step could be helping students identify the physical symptoms that precede a reaction, like sweaty palms, a heated face, or a quaking voice. Eventually, students can learn to anticipate their triggers and proactively circumnavigate the inciting event.

In order for students to address the problem of a lack of mindfulness and self-awareness, they must learn the difference between reacting and responding. Start with how important it is to think before acting, and try giving them a tool to fall back on in the heat of the moment. For this, you can use the acronym PLAN:

- PAUSE. Stop what you're doing, as if you've been caught in a game of Freeze Tag, and engage in mindful breathing. Close your eyes. Take five deep breaths, inflating your stomach like a balloon each time. For especially intense reactions, it can be helpful to inhale and hold to the count of four, then exhale and hold to the count of four, and repeat.

- LISTEN. What is your body trying to tell you? Allow your body to speak to you by noticing, without judgment, both your emotions and your physical symptoms. What happens in your body in the seconds after you've been provoked? What thoughts flood your mind? Notice these thoughts and feelings, but don't cling to them. Let them come and go as you breathe and listen.

- **ASK.** Is what your body telling you to do (the reaction) a true representation of who you want to be as a person? What choice could you make that you would be proud to remember tomorrow? How can you honor your values with your response? Will your reaction bring harm to the community?

- **NEXT.** Decide what to do. You've taken a moment to breathe, acknowledge how you feel, and reconnect to your values. You're much more likely now to make a decision you won't regret. Take the next step to move through the conflict without infringing upon the well-being of your classroom and school community.

One of our favorite strategies to help make these abstract ideas more concrete for students is to use Calm Down Jars. Fill a glass jar half with water and half with hand soap, and sprinkle in glitter. Hot glue the lid, and you have yourself a Calm Down Jar. When the jar is shaken, the glitter swirls around. Explain that this is what the student's mind looks like when it's chasing after dozens of thoughts and emotions. Slowly watch the glitter fall to the bottom of the jar. As it does, practice mindful breathing. Once the glitter has settled, show the students how much more clear the water is—just as their minds become more clear with stillness and deep breathing.

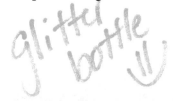

Try having a Calm Down Jar available for students to use when they feel frustrated. This tool isn't just for our younger students, either. Though they may roll their eyes at first, big kids love glitter as much as little ones do. In fact, we once had a high school student ask for a pass to our classroom just so she could "check out" the Calm Down Jar for the rest of the period.

WHAT YOU CAN DO TOMORROW

No single lesson plan or strategy will transform your students into masters of their thoughts, emotions, and responses overnight, but even small steps toward mindfulness can make a difference in the classroom culture.

- **UNCOVER STUDENTS' VALUES.** If you asked your students to name the three most important things to them, most would probably include belongings like their cell phones and gaming consoles. Kids are inundated with the message that possessions are our most valuable assets. Imagine the culture we could build if students valued each other the most. Try redirecting them by having them examine the characteristics, habits, and personality traits that they most admire, instead of possessions.

  First, ask them to think of someone they admire. This could be a family member, friend, or celebrity, but it should be someone who represents the kind of person the student wants to become. Ask students to describe this person in writing. This can be just a simple, jotted-down list.

Next, have students examine their own legacies. Ask, "If you were to move tomorrow, how would you want your friends to remember you? What about people who didn't know you well? What words would you want others to use to describe you to someone you have never met?" Again, ask students to record their thoughts.

Once complete, invite students to compare these lists. What are the common threads? Ask them to spend three or four minutes silently reflecting on what these lists say about the kinds of characteristics, habits, and traits they value. After a few minutes of independent reflection, give students the opportunity to talk in small groups.

You may want to provide students with a list of values in case they need help articulating their ideas. Explain that the list is not comprehensive and is only a guide. This will be especially helpful for the students who are struggling to make connections between their lists.

The goal is for each student to select three to five qualities they hope to embody–their values. Circle up and have students share those values. Discuss the types of choices they can make to live their values out loud. Moving forward, refer back to these values to help students problem-solve and resolve conflict.

The next task is to create a visual reminder of these values. If the students have classroom notebooks, they could record their values on the front covers. You could create a wall sign for your class (or each class period) that represents the students' values.

You'll find it useful to connect values and expectations. Reexamine the classroom expectations. What do they say about what you value as a class?

• **STRENGTHEN THE MIND-BODY CONNECTION.** At one point or another, we all have been overcome by emotion only to receive the age-old advice of "get over it," as if there were on/off switches for shaking hands, upset stomachs, and tense muscles. Emotions manifest into physical sensations, which can compound the intensity of the experience. When students understand the way their bodies physically react to emotion, they become more self-aware and recover more quickly.

You can discuss this separately or integrate it into morning circles. As students discuss how they're feeling, ask them to talk about what's happening physically, as well. Have other students share what happens to them when they feel especially angry, excited, frightened, or important. Physical symptoms can serve as early warning signs that a student needs to stop, breathe, and think before he acts. For example, a student might note that when he's angry, his heart races. By becoming more sensitive to the early stress signals of his body, he might come to realize that his heart starts racing before his mind recognizes that he is feeling frustrated. With practice, this can be his cue to stop, breathe, and think so that his next step is a response, not a reaction.

We want our students to be resilient and bounce back quickly, so we have to teach them how to recover. If a student is aware that her muscles remain tense after an argument, she can practice relaxing them by tightening and then releasing, soothing her sympathetic nervous system. A student who feels overheated might choose on his own to splash cool water on his face if he understands that it will actually help him feel better. Understanding the mind-body connection can help students recover more quickly and let go of their emotions, instead of bottling them up, only to explode later.

- **MODEL EMPATHY IN THE MOMENT.** As they say, the students who act least deserving of our love are often the ones who need it the most. It can be hard to balance the maintenance of personal rela-tionships with students and the maintenance of classroom expectations. Since the expectations are dependent upon the relationships, though, address the person before the problem.

Say you have a student walk in late, slam his books on his desk, and immediately pull out his cell phone. The whole class stops, waiting to see how you will handle the situation. Model empathy by choosing not to react. Instead, finish setting up the activity or wrap up the lecture, then go to that student's side. Before reprimanding the student for coming in late, disrupting the class, and breaking the cell phone policy (which go against your classroom expectations of creating a safe space where all students can learn and engage in productive work), start by asking the student how he is feeling. Often, a simple, non-accusatory "Hey, what's up?" is enough to prompt the student to talk.

If he's reluctant to share, you might start with an observation. "It looks like you might be angry. Can you tell me more about that?" This can help you uncover what's behind the behavior. Remember, outbursts and attitudes are rarely manipulative schemes. That student probably did not wake up that morning and decide he would walk in late and disrupt your lesson on the Battle of Waterloo. Once you have taken appropriate steps to address the student as a person, then you can work on restoring the classroom expectations.

- **STRESS THE IMPORTANCE OF SELF-CARE.** Yes, it's true that young people tend to be naturally self-centered. But while they may spend a great deal of time thinking about themselves, they might not know how to actually take care of themselves. We know students (like adults) spend hours engaged in mindless activities, like video games, social media, and watching television. These activities look relaxing on the surface, but certainly aren't replenishing.

Encourage students to become more mindful of how they spend their time. Ask your students to create a timeline of the day before, and list each thing they did that day. Next, ask the students to sort their lists into three categories: replenishing, relaxing, and draining. An activity is replenishing if it leaves the student feeling revitalized, zestful, and ready to tackle whatever lies ahead. Replenishing activities might include exercising, volunteering, or crafting. An activity is relaxing if it helps the student feel calm, but not necessarily re-energized. This could include coloring, listening to music, or watching television. An activity is draining if the students dread it and it leaves them feeling tired and annoyed. This likely includes homework and chores.

Next, ask students to examine the balance of their day. Was it mostly full of replenishing, relaxing, or draining activities? Sure, many draining activities are necessary parts of life, and these are often the activities that lead to our growth and success. Draining activities can't be cut out, but they can be counterbalanced by replenishing activities. Though it's nice to relax, and time should be devoted to relaxation, the true antidote to feeling run-down is to do the things that fill us with life.

Encourage students to create a list of things they find replenishing. You might start by sharing some of your own, and then brainstorming as a class. This could also be a good small-circle activity. Once students have decent lists, ask them to look at their weekly agendas and mindfully schedule time for replenishment. While they're at it, go ahead and schedule some for yourself as well.

A BLUEPRINT FOR FULL IMPLEMENTATION

In order for students to be aware of their emotions and the difference between reacting and responding, they must be able to talk about their emotions freely and often. A key to making mindfulness the norm for students in your class is to incorporate strategies in your daily and weekly routines. These strategies will help you keep mindfulness going throughout the year.

STEP 1: Normalize emotions.

It can be uncomfortable for students to openly discuss emotions. The more we normalize these conversations, the more open students will be to exploring and articulating their own feelings.

It's important for students to feel safe expressing a wide range of emotions, so we want to reinforce that all feelings are valid. There are not "good feelings" and "bad feelings"; each feeling has its place and serves its purpose. Students should not judge themselves for how they feel, as this will only lead to negative self-talk.

You can start by modeling this. In your morning circles, ask how everyone is feeling, and lead by example. "Today, I am feeling frustrated. My dog would not come inside when it was time for me to leave, and I was late getting to work." As students become more comfortable identifying their emotions, you can add a "so what" to this reflection: "I am letting this morning's frustration go by taking deep breaths and keeping things in perspective. Being a few minutes late to work isn't the end of the world, especially if it rarely happens."

These morning circle reflections can be just what students need to vent their stress so that they don't carry it with them throughout the day, and this open dialogue can lead to discussions that promote problem-solving and empathizing.

STEP 2: Make a habit of mindful breathing.

Start each morning circle with one minute of mindful breathing. Students might interpret this as trying to clear their minds of thought, but that isn't the case. (As teachers, we want our students to do more thinking, not less.) Explain that the goal of mindful breathing isn't to get rid of their thoughts, but to teach their minds to let thoughts and feelings come and go without getting lost in them. You might ask if anyone in the class has been in a good mood until one negative thought suddenly carried it away and ruined the good vibes. The objective isn't necessarily to control our thoughts and feelings during mindful breathing, but to teach ourselves not to let those thoughts and feelings control us.

Remind students as they breathe to notice their thoughts without getting carried away by them. They can visualize their thoughts as clouds passing in the sky or as leaves floating down a stream. Explain that when they notice their minds wandering, they can simply note it by thinking "wandering" and then refocus on their breath, letting go of the thought or feeling just as they would let go of the cloud or the leaf. The goal here is not to stop their minds from wandering. It is to help them reconnect to the present moment and not get carried away by their thoughts and emotions.

You can also incorporate mindful breathing into your transitions. When switching from one activity to the next, stop for thirty seconds of mindful breathing. This can help students switch gears and reset before moving on. Once students have mastered the mindful breathing transitions, consider adding simple stretches to match the breathing. The combination of deep breathing and stretching helps clear any stress hormones that might have started to accumulate during work, so that they feel refreshed to move on.

STEP 3: Override negativity bias.

Students are probably already somewhat aware of the negativity bias, even if they don't yet have the language to isolate and name it. Ask them if they remember the last five criticisms they received. Then ask them if they remember the last five compliments.

Chances are, they will recall the negative feedback more quickly than the positive. It isn't that students are abnormally pessimistic; the human brain is wired to pay more attention to the negative than the positive. Awareness of this bias and a focused effort to override it can create more optimistic students who are less stressed and more likely to respond than to react. This also leads to smoother conflict resolution. Acknowledging that it is easier to focus on the "bad" in another person than it is to remember the "good" can help students put their disagreements into perspective.

You can promote positive thinking in many ways. A common practice is to write in a daily gratitude journal. Incorporate it into the morning circle to set the tone for the day. Another strategy is to delve into moments of positivity. Does the student finally understand the difference between dominant and recessive genes? Awesome! Don't diminish the accomplishment by rushing on to the next task. Allow the student to focus on his success and the good feelings it brings. If your students are nervous before a quiz, ask them to recall a time when they did well and try to bring up those emotions. This may only take an extra minute or two, but it helps train the brain to associate challenge with the rewarding feeling of accomplishment.

OVERCOMING PUSHBACK

Students might find it strange when you ask them to talk about their emotions and engage in mindful breathing at school. Shouldn't they be spending their time actually learning? You might find your colleagues and administration asking you that question, too. Here are tips for overcoming pushback.

YOU'RE A TEACHER, NOT A THERAPIST. OR, I CAME HERE TO LEARN, NOT TALK ABOUT MY FEELINGS. Don't be surprised to hear this, especially in the early stages of your restorative discipline journey. You're asking your students to be vulnerable. You're inviting their whole selves to the classroom, when for years, only their academic selves found a seat at the table. Be patient. Explain to students, colleagues, and administration that academic success is at the heart of this work. Reassure students that yes, they are, in fact, at school to learn. Your job as their teacher is to give them the best set of circumstances for learning to happen. A healthy, calm mind is much better prepared to learn than one weighed down by stress or loneliness. A safe, empathetic environment is more conducive to learning than one where students are afraid to fail in front of one another. The better equipped students are to handle their emotions, the more time they can spend during the day actively engaged in learning instead of getting wrapped up in drama.

TEACHERS HAVE BEEN TELLING ME TO JUST TAKE A DEEP BREATH FOR YEARS, AND IT NEVER WORKS. To their credit, "take a deep breath" is a pretty cliché solution to the overwhelming emotions flooding their bodies. They might have tried it once or twice, not felt immediate nirvana, and tossed it in the can with the rest of the Things Adults Say That Don't Work.

We've found that the more students understand the science, the biology, behind the power of deep breathing, the more they're willing to stick with it beyond the first exasperated huffs. The depth of this exploration depends on the development and interest of your students. You could simply explain that when a person feels stressed or angry, his body perceives this as a danger and goes into fight or flight mode. Taking deep breaths helps calm his nervous system so his body knows it's safe to slow his heart rate, lower his blood pressure, and clear out those hormones that flooded his angry muscles.

If your students are interested in learning more (or if you have an especially reluctant practitioner), consider having them research the relationship between their sympathetic and parasympathetic nervous systems or the hormones that control how a person copes with various emotions. Once students see that deep breathing isn't just some wishy-washy platitude that annoying adults throw around, they might stick with it long enough to watch it work for themselves.

THE HACK IN ACTION
Leigh walks into class with a scowl, sits in the back, and puts her head down. As the rest of the class trickles in, the teacher overhears whispers about Leigh's argument with her math teacher, Mr. Bruns, the class before. Apparently, Leigh had been removed from class and was scheduled for a restorative circle tomorrow before school. It is still early in the day, though, and Leigh has four classes to get through yet. If she isn't able to manage how she is feeling, it will certainly be a wasted day academically, and she will more than likely end up in trouble in another class.

The bell rings, and the students take their seats in the circle they formed as they came in. Miss Dubois welcomes the students, and they start their daily practice of opening with mindful breathing. Miss Dubois is relieved to see Leigh participate, even if her exhales are a little more huffy than usual. Going around the circle, students have the chance to share what's on their minds, and when one student mentions that he's nervous about tomorrow's math test, Leigh visibly tenses.

When the talking piece makes its way to Leigh, she hesitates, but then drops her shoulders. "I'm really mad right now. I didn't have my math homework and it's the second assignment I missed this week, but only the third assignment in the last six weeks. Mr. Bruns went off on me about how my work ethic is slipping and I need to check my priorities. He was acting like I never do my work, so I told him "whatever." Then he told me to go in the hall and I snapped. He didn't need to make it that big of a deal and blow it all out of proportion. He was flipping out for no reason, and I told him so. Now I have to deal with my parents when I get home and go to a circle tomorrow morning."

Miss Dubois nods. Reminding herself to address the person before the problem, she offers her empathy. "It sounds like you were really frustrated. You're usually a reliable student, so I can understand why having your work ethic questioned would be upsetting."

Leigh half nods, half shrugs. "Yeah. He was in the wrong but then I snapped, so now I'm in trouble."

"That is unfortunate. I wonder how this could have turned out differently," Miss Dubois prompts.

Leigh sighs and rolls her eyes, but resignation and validation are present in her response, not disrespect. "I should have PLANned. I felt my face getting hot as soon as Mr. Bruns started talking, but I didn't stop to take a breath. I just let myself get mad and go off and now I have to deal with my parents and this circle when I could have just sat there and talked to him when I wasn't as mad."

The circle discussion concludes with the other students offering Leigh empathy and cracking jokes to ease her tension. The class moves on, and because she was given the chance to work through how she felt, Leigh is able to actively participate.

We went into teaching because we wanted to teach students, not because we wanted to teach science, and that means we have to invite the whole student into our classrooms. Caring for the whole student means going beyond the content. Students need to be taught the skills to manage their emotions, just as they need to be taught how to read the periodic table. Mindfulness practices support restorative discipline by creating self-awareness and empowering students to take ownership of managing their emotions.

CULTIVATE EMPATHY
BUILD THE CAPACITY TO LISTEN, UNDERSTAND, AND COMMUNICATE

You never really understand a person until you consider things from his point of view ... until you climb inside of his skin and walk around in it.

—ATTICUS FINCH, IN HARPER LEE'S *TO KILL A MOCKINGBIRD*

THE PROBLEM: STUDENTS DON'T SPEAK THE LANGUAGE OF EMPATHY

HAVING STUDENTS LEARN from their actions, repair harm that they have caused, and empathize with others are critical components of restorative justice. Empathy means sharing and understanding the emotions of others, and it is made up of three pieces. A gap in any one can be counterproductive to the learning environment. First, affectual empathy is the ability to feel the emotions with the other person, like feeling embarrassed with a friend when she trips on the ice. Next, cognitive empathy is the ability to recognize and understand the emotions of others without feeling the emotion itself. Therapists understand their patients' emotions, but it would be unhealthy and counterproductive if they felt them as well. Last, emotional regulation determines the type of empathetic reactions we display.

Today's high-tech world gives us the opportunity to communicate across borders, time zones, and cultures. Never before has it been more convenient to connect with others. But the face of interaction is changing, and many teachers note the effects in their classrooms. Because so many students are "plugging in" as soon as they get home instead of gathering in backyards or on playgrounds, today's kids have less in-person socialization and fewer opportunities to learn how to read facial expressions, body language, and tone of voice. Kids who are ineffective at reading and understanding the emotions of others can exhibit seemingly inappropriate and immature behaviors because they are not able to communicate in an effective way.

Students who have a hard time reading others can also have a hard time noticing the impact of their own behavior, or anticipating it, which can lead to frustrating moments in the classroom for students and the teacher.

One example is when students struggle when they engage in collaborative work. Their approaches may be more self-serving than diplomatic, impeding upon others' learning and invalidating their contributions. Collaboration is one of the most important skills for success in school at any level, but especially for college and career readiness. Students who struggle in this area may have a harder time being a team player, which later can limit their career opportunities.

Bullying can be another symptom of an empathy gap. Students

who don't empathize might laugh at or mock their peers, especially when the other kids express emotions that could be interpreted as weakness. The instigator will transfer the blame to the victim with statements like, "You're too sensitive. I was just playing." This can lead to an emotionally unsafe learning environment where students are so afraid of the criticism of an unempathetic peer that they shut down and refuse to take risks, limiting the ability to embrace a growth mindset.

More symptoms can include manipulative behaviors, jealousy, refusal to admit wrongdoing, entitlement, and the inability to consider other perspectives. None of these characteristics creates a healthy learning environment, and they all get in the way of successfully implementing restorative justice. Thankfully, the ability to empathize is not purely genetic. Empathy is a muscle that can be strengthened with the right set of tools.

THE HACK: CULTIVATE EMPATHY

We must be intentional about cultivating empathy in our classrooms. Many students are not hardwired to understand others. Empathy must be learned and practiced. Not all students get exposure to people who are different than them, or have had opportunities to learn to interact successfully with people who are different than them. These students will fall behind on the path toward empathy, just from a lack of exposure.

Empathy must be present, however, if you want an emotionally safe learning space where students can be themselves, take risks, and speak freely, without fear of ridicule and judgment, and where bad behavior is minimized because students are better able to empathize with others.

The first step in fostering empathy is to give students the tools to recognize social cues and the feelings of others. Students also need to become aware of how their own communication styles and choices affect other people. Start incorporating the ideas in your classroom that empathetic body language, tone, and diction are aspects of communication.

Expose your students to people and ideas that are outside of their normal everyday experiences to help them connect with the wider world around them and demystify the different results in students who are more empathetic, compassionate, and invested in their communities. It always surprises us to learn, three or four weeks into the year, that students still don't know each other's names. Although the class might work within the classroom, we don't always take into account how much students are actually reaching across different social circles in the class and outside of it. Try walking students through exercises to examine who is in their social circles, who isn't, and why. Talk about ways to build additional relationships and regularly follow up to ask what the students have learned about each other. Inviting students to get to know different social circles within their immediate classroom environment will set them on the path of learning empathy in a safe place.

HELP YOUR STUDENTS DEVELOP BROADER EMPATHY BY CONNECTING THEM WITH PEOPLE THEY NORMALLY MAY NOT ENCOUNTER.

Expanding their circles goes beyond the classroom. How often do your students have the chance to explore the world beyond themselves? Do they have regular opportunities to build relationships with people of varying socioeconomic backgrounds, ethnicities, religions, ages, and cultures? It's easy to judge and even fear the unfamiliar. Help your students develop broader empathy by connecting them with people they normally may not encounter. Invite community members to your classroom to share their stories, and so your students can tell theirs. Use technology to connect with people across town, across the country, and across the world. Encourage students to explore their similarities for a deeper sense of shared humanity. Also encourage them to explore their differences and, instead of fearing them, embrace the fact that our differences create a richer world and do not have to put us at odds with each other.

WHAT YOU CAN DO TOMORROW

Start by teaching empathetic communication techniques. It helps to begin with concrete aspects of body language and syntax. Students can then learn the subtleties of active and reflective listening.

- **BODY LANGUAGE.** We know that our body language communicates just as much as, if not more than, our words and tone. The wrong body language can completely undermine our best intentions and derail an otherwise productive conversation. To set the stage for active listening and respectful dialogue, make students more cognizant of the nonverbal messages they're sending.

  Teach simple body language interpretation by examining photos and matching the corresponding emotion or message. Role-playing can also be helpful. Ask for four volunteers. Seat two volunteers at the front of the room, facing each other but turned slightly toward the class. Seat the other two off to either side. Give all four volunteers a copy of a script. The students who are off to the side will be the voices of the students seated in the front.

As the speakers read the script, ask the seated volunteers to act as if they are speaking, but focus on communicating a specific message with their body language. Complete another round, but have the seated volunteers choose a different emotion to represent with their body language. The idea is that the speakers who read the script keep a consistent tone between each round so that the words and tone remain the same, but the message is received differently because of changes in body language.

Have the rest of the class record their observations, and then facilitate a discussion about how changes in body language affected the message. If your students already have a basic understanding of empathy, they can discuss how different positions and gestures communicated (or didn't communicate) empathy.

Also, encourage students to practice mindful body language. Remind them at the beginning of your morning circle that their peers are counting on them to be active participants and open listeners, and that the first step is receptive body language. Model sitting with your head up, shoulders relaxed, and good posture. Avoid crossing your arms or making impatient or otherwise negative facial expressions. (Or, do just the opposite and ask students how your body language changes the way they interpret your attitude and investment in the circle.)

As the circle proceeds, give students who maintain welcoming body language positive affirmations. Encourage students to maintain eye contact with the speaker. This can be especially unnerving, so reassure them that it will probably feel more natural with practice. (And if not, they will at least get better at covering their nerves.)

Positive reinforcement also works when students are collaborating in small groups. You might create a special gesture that indicates, "Hey! Great body language!" so you don't disrupt the flow of conversation. Small groups are also an opportunity to improve students' self-awareness. A student might be tired or stressed and fail to realize that his body language is communicating disinterest or annoyance. Establishing a gesture that means, "Check your body language" can be a non-confrontational way to increase students' awareness. If the student does not pick up on the gesture, check in with the student and remind her that her peers will react to body language without even realizing they're doing so.

Body language is an important component of active listening, as well. Offer students the chance to practice mindful body language with various adults to better prepare for job interviews and internships. One activity to build empathy among students and staff and allow students to practice effective listening is to ask students to interview teachers, custodial staff, cafeteria employees, front-office workers, and any other adults in the building whom they regularly encounter but rarely engage in conversation. Students can practice their interviews with each other while you provide guidance to help them avoid fidgeting, drumming fingers, or glancing at the clock. Nodding and offering brief acknowledgment responses ("uh-huh," "right") reassures the listener that you are actively engaged in the conversation.

- **AFFECTIVE STATEMENTS.** The use of affective statements, also known as *I statements*, can improve communication and foster empathy by reducing defensiveness, avoiding blame, and encouraging students to take personal responsibility through self-awareness. Affective statements follow this formula: I feel_____ when_____ because_____.

Model affective statements by sharing examples on the board. Remember that this technique isn't reserved for negative experiences; feel free to model a variety of emotions. You can move forward by having students make suggestions. Ask a volunteer to share an emotion, then another volunteer to share the event, and another volunteer to provide the context. Allowing students to be silly will help lower their resistance when it's time for them to create their own statements.

A possible "we do" next step could be having students pair up and create affective statements for fictional characters. You could do this by reflecting on recent readings, having students read short children's books, showing clips from movies, or showing commercials. This can be especially helpful because it calls on students to practice affective statements and empathize with characters by considering the characters' perspectives and how the characters are affected by others in the story.

As an alternative, provide students with a list of sentences to rewrite as affective statements. (Example: "You made me mad because you were rude on the playground" could be turned into "I felt angry when you cut in front of me in line for the swings because I had been waiting my turn for a while.")

Once students understand how to craft affective statements, make this a regular part of your circles.

- **REFLECTIVE LISTENING.** We're all guilty of it sometimes: Instead of actively listening, we're busy preparing our own responses in our minds, daydreaming, or thinking of all the reasons the other person is wrong. Instead of empathizing, we're focusing on our own thoughts or feelings. Help your students communicate more attentively by teaching them reflective listening, especially during restorative circles, when emotions can run high.

  Reflective listening is the process of allowing one person to speak while the other listens attentively. Once the first point has been made, the speaker pauses and allows the listener to reflect back what they heard. This reassures the speaker that he or she is being heard and understood, and allows the listener to ask clarifying questions.

Structure:

- Speaker A speaks while Speaker B listens. Encourage Speaker A to use affective statements.

- Speaker B reflects back what they heard from Speaker A. "I think I heard you say _____. Is that correct, and did I miss anything?"

Example:

Speaker A: "I felt disappointed when you went back on your promise to get the car fixed. I was overwhelmed last week because of holiday preparation and Charlie's illness. Getting the car fixed was the only thing I asked you to help with, and when you didn't get it done, I felt unappreciated. In the future, I need you to please keep your promises or be upfront when you aren't sure you can follow through."

Speaker B: "I think I'm hearing that you felt unappreciated and frustrated when I didn't get the car fixed last week, after promising to do so. You had a lot on your plate already, and you need to know that you can rely on me when I say I'll do something. Is that right, and did I miss anything?"

This forces Speaker B to carefully listen to Speaker A in order to summarize. This is not the time to daydream or prepare a defense. It also ensures Speaker A that Speaker B is listening and expressing the ideas clearly. If Speaker B hasn't understood correctly, this gives Speaker A the chance to clarify things before continuing.

A BLUEPRINT FOR FULL IMPLEMENTATION

Building empathy with students is not an event; it is a continual process that will need to be reinforced through intentional curriculum, and through situations where you can use restorative practices. The following blueprint will help you build a culture of empathy that will enhance the learning environment of your classroom.

STEP 1: Actively reject stereotypes.

Stereotypes strip people of their individuality and promote "us vs. them" thinking. Viewing someone as "other" creates distance and even indifference. Foster empathy in your students by actively dispelling stereotypes. Sometimes, we hear students making jokes that we know are inappropriate, but it's easier to ignore than address, especially when we overhear these jokes in the hallway during passing period or while roaming the lunchroom during cafeteria duty. If we want to create empathetic learners who will go on to become fair and equitable leaders, though, we cannot pass up these teachable moments.

Stereotypes are more than hurtful; they can also be harmful. Gender stereotypes pigeonhole girls as inferior athletes and underperforming mathematicians. Girls might be so afraid of confirming these stereotypes that they simply avoid the situation. Boys can be stereotyped as hyper-masculine, and feel pressured to bottle up their emotions or avoid pursuing interests that others might label as "girly." Racial stereotyping has a negative impact on academic achievement and test performance. Students who believe they are expected to perform poorly do not do as well as those whose abilities are reaffirmed by their peers and their teachers.

Make it a habit to confront stereotypes, no matter the context.

Actively reject stereotypes in your classroom by addressing jokes and comments that you overhear. Even if you know it wasn't intended to be malicious, don't condone the use of slurs by ignoring them. Instead of approaching this work with a punitive or shaming mindset, embrace the opportunity to help your students understand the impact their words can have on those around them. Have an open, honest conversation about how stereotypes are started and perpetuated, but more important, how your students can stop the cycle.

STEP 2: Humanize the curriculum.

No matter what grade level or content area you teach, do your best to bring the human experience into your classroom as often as you can. Go beyond the typical textbook coverage and include, instead, lessons about people from all walks of life. In geometry, discuss the ancient Egyptians and the pyramids. Connect your study of magnetism to that done in ancient China. Explore the stories of Nikola Tesla and Elijah McCoy and how they became the engineers whose work continues to shape our lives. Behind every lesson in every content area is a face, a story, and a chance for students to connect their experiences to the broader world.

STEP 3: Bring culture to the classroom.

Welcoming the whole student into your classroom means creating opportunities for students to share their home cultures, and not just when a special designation on the calendar says it's time. Your students can take the lead in shaping how this happens. Most students will jump at the chance to showcase something about their culture that isn't commercially recognized or traditionally validated at school.

If you need jumping-off points, consider the following:

- Invite students to tell the stories of their families. Be sensitive to those who may not have this information by offering everyone the alternative of adopting a famous family.

- Ask students who speak other languages to teach the class how to recite the date or something relevant to the curriculum.

- Host a potluck and ask students to contribute a favorite family dish.

- Incorporate traditional dances or other elements of cultural festivals.

Many resources are available to help you develop a multicultural classroom, and the best resource is your students.

STEP 4: Teach what empathy isn't.

We want our students to care, but we don't want them to take on everyone else's problems. Part of effectively empathizing is respecting the needs of the listener. Warn students to avoid the following common pitfalls:

FIXING. Remind students that it's not their responsibility to fix other people's problems. Sure, they can offer their help, but the burden should not fall on their shoulders. How can a student know if someone wants help fixing a problem? Take the guesswork out and encourage students to ask how best they can support each other. "Do you just need to vent? Or would you like to brainstorm solutions together?"

UNSOLICITED ADVICE. Students might confuse being empathetic with just plain being nosy. Remind them to respect others' privacy and not to insert themselves into other people's conversations or problems (unless, of course, they're doing so to prevent real harm). No one likes to receive unsolicited advice, and it's rarely helpful and often damaging to the relationship.

DISMISSING/MINIMIZING. Part of an empathetic response is the desire to make the other person feel better. A student might be tempted to do this by trying to convince his classmate that it "isn't a big deal." In spite of the reassuring intent, this response invalidates the experience of the other person and can cause shame and guilt.

OVERCOMING PUSHBACK

The increasing prevalence of technology offers endless platforms for people to speak their minds and share their opinions. The other side of the coin is that (most of the time) anyone who disagrees has access to the same platform. This results in battles and debates over the freedom of speech and political correctness. Here are concerns that could create pushback to instilling empathy, and strategies to ensure that you acknowledge everyone's voice.

LIGHTEN UP. NO ONE CAN TAKE A JOKE ANYMORE. You might hear this from a student (or the parent of a student) who has been redirected for making a joke that perpetuates a stereotype or for using slurs in non-confrontational social situations. Be prepared to talk to parents and students about the negative academic impact of stereotypes and learning environments that feel unsafe or unwelcoming. Your job is to create a classroom where all learners are safe and supported.

HERE COME THE POLITICAL CORRECTNESS POLICE. Students love to repeat what they hear on television or see online, and reject anything that limits their freedom of expression and individuality. They might equate your expectation of respectful speaking and listening with forcing political correctness. Reassure students that they are free to express their thoughts and opinions—with the expectation that they do so with respect and kindness. Unpopular opinions are welcome; impoliteness isn't.

THE HACK IN ACTION

"Seriously, every time I look at Mr. Costa, he yells at me. He hates me, and I didn't even do anything to him!" said Allen as he was talking to me about his study hall.

This was a common theme of my conversations with this student. Allen's most frequent behaviors were classroom distractions, being off-task, and insubordination.

I facilitated a restorative mediation with Mr. Costa and Allen to figure out what has been going on and to repair the harm. I first asked Mr. Costa to go through what had been going on in the study hall. Mr. Costa stated, "Well, Allen loves attention. He walks into class with his headphones so loud the entire class can hear it. He refuses to pull out his laptop and work, and when I redirect him to take out his laptop, he will just completely refuse to work. I ask him again, and he will even walk out of the study hall sometimes. It's completely unacceptable, Allen."

I then posed the same question to Allen, and he stated, "I

always have my headphones loud. My laptop was dead yesterday, and I didn't have a charger. You didn't ask me to work; you just yelled at me. The second time you said something, I walked out so I wouldn't say anything stupid. I think I did good."

I then asked Allen, "How do you think Mr. Costa feels when he has a quiet study hall and a student walks in with headphones loud enough the entire class can hear it?"

"I don't know," Allen said. "Probably mad if it was already quiet."

"It just causes a lot of disruption and stirs people up some," Mr. Costa stated. "I just want it to be a good learning environment for everyone."

"Didn't think about that," Allen continued, looking down at the table and fidgeting with a pencil.

"Can you explain to me why you didn't tell Mr. Costa your laptop was dead yesterday, and that you didn't have a charger?" I continued to drive the mediation.

"He should have known because it wasn't on," Allen mumbled.

"Allen, I couldn't tell, and I didn't know that. I also had to talk very loudly for you to hear me due to your headphones being so loud," Mr. Costa said firmly.

I quickly jumped in with, "Thanks for sharing that, Mr. Costa. Allen thought you were yelling at him when he paused his music."

"If I didn't have my headphones so loud, I would have heard you. I should have asked to borrow a charger," Allen replied.

This mediation allowed Allen and Mr. Costa to see each other's perspective, have an open dialogue around the conflict, and discuss next steps. Gaining perspective is one of the main components in developing empathy. Now that they both have an insight into their displaying behaviors—teacher speaking loudly and student "refusing" to work—they both have better ways to work together during study hall.

Restorative discipline relies on the investment of the community and its commitment to everyone's well-being. Students who have empathy for each other care about the culture of their classroom and the impact their behavior has on that culture. Fostering empathy reduces conflict and also makes conflict resolution easier when problems do arise.

BUILD RESTORATIVE SUPPORT
FOCUS ON THE SMALL THINGS

To become a strategist—and not just a tactician—look towards the future, think about growth, and start communicating those ideas with smart people around you.

—JENNIFER RENDANT, EDUCATION AND
STRATEGIC COMMUNICATIONS SPECIALIST

THE PROBLEM: SCHOOLWIDE POLICIES ARE NOT ENOUGH

HOW CAN WE, as educators, make an impact on student performance in our buildings? We hear from a lot of educators who attend professional development training on new evidence-based practices, hoping they're going to be game-changers. They believe administrators will develop the practices into schoolwide policies, and boom! School climate will be improved. They quickly realize, though, that it was a false expectation.

Here's the problem: policies that address the entire school often miss individual students and cases. And each miss is another behavior that goes unaddressed.

Many schools adopt the solution of Multi-Tiered System of Supports (also known as MTSS), a popular framework in which schools use data-based decision-making for interventions and plans of action to address student performance. Using MTSS tools and strategies, faculties analyze data on a daily basis then apply the information to pinpoint areas of potential weakness for each student. Typically, the goals of Multi-Tiered System of Supports policies are to help schools and districts align academic standards and behavioral expectations in order to improve student performance. As the name implies, they use several tiers of information:

TIER 1. Tier 1 is defined as the universal interventions that educators give in all settings and to all students. They focus on being preventive and proactive by encouraging student success through progress monitoring. Between 80 and 90 percent of your student body will fall into this tier. Tier 1 uses high-quality classroom management delivered through universal design and accommodations.

TIER 2. Tier 2 interventions are more targeted, and typically affect 15 to 20 percent of your student population. This tier is where educators utilize selected standardized interventions, individualized monitoring, and individualized assessments. Needless to say, the more effective these interventions, the fewer complex Tier 3 approaches students will need.

TIER 3. Tier 3 interventions are intensive and include 3 to 5 percent of your students. These students should have heavily individualized approaches to their learning, and these may include modifications and accommodations as deemed appropriate by specialists, health professionals, and administrators.

The overarching thought process of MTSS should be to accurately identify student deficits, barriers, and soft-skill goals in regard to social and emotional learning. Multi-Tiered System of Supports helps drive effective classroom environments for students. The framework of MTSS should include preventive measures, tailored restorative intervention, and targeted logical and need-based interventions.

However, MTSS can be one of those highly anticipated game-changers that, in all reality, might not be the most effective way to enhance overall school climate on its own. School climate isn't built through better policies. It's built through better relationships.

Universal policies are often too rigid and do not focus on building and improving crucial relationships throughout the school. It is difficult for systems like MTSS to individualize supports, especially regarding student behavior needs. Take into account that many students need social-emotional interventions, for example. MTSS may help address large gaps in student performance, but it may not help deduce which students need that extra social or emotional support.

MTSS models can also result in the labeling and pigeonholing of students, and the interventions do not always work for everyone. This is hard to combat when creating a schoolwide approach, but you can account for this by allowing students to repair the harm as a form of intervention. When students use restorative practices, they are able to maintain their sense of community with their classmates.

Building restorative discipline into your MTSS model allows for the support needed for social-emotional variables and unique student needs. Increasing these factors readjusts MTSS to be more of a support model than a labeling model when someone is struggling.

THE HACK: BUILD RESTORATIVE SUPPORT

School climate is built around relationships, but relationships are tough to develop, especially during and after conflict. Restorative practices allow teachers and administrators to hold students accountable, develop an inclusive school climate, and maintain and strengthen relationships. Try implementing restorative practices into your Multi-Tiered System of Supports with the following ideas:

TIER 1. Since Tier 1 involves universal interventions for all learners and school environments, how do we implement restorative discipline in Tier 1?

- Use restorative language throughout the building.

- Practice circles to create a culture of restorative practices.

- Create clear and consistent expectations.

TIER 2. Tier 2 interventions are more targeted, so the restorative discipline component should be strongly utilized when conflicts present themselves. How can we add restorative practices within this MTSS tier?

- Execute restorative mediations on a regular basis.

- Allow students to participate in decision-making and repair the harm.

- Reach and encourage growth mindset thinking.

TIER 3. As the most intensive interventions, Tier 3 supports are already individualized. To implement restorative discipline at this stage in the process, your school culture will need to embrace effective, data-based practices, such as:

- Create an empathy-driven culture.

- Encourage mindfulness in all students and staff.

- Adopt a "relationships first" motto.

Nothing will completely overcome the individualized behavioral and need deficits in each student; too much complexity exists around each student's barriers, emotional development, and backgrounds. MTSS is simply a problem-solving tool. With restorative discipline integrated every step of the way, however, a positive climate becomes achievable. Together, the two practices will collaboratively *enhance* classroom culture, school climate, and student productivity.

WHAT YOU CAN DO TOMORROW

Any school that utilizes MTSS will tell you that it takes time, practice, and collaboration to implement. Adding in restorative practices probably feels as though it will take your team forever to improve school climate. Our best recommendation is to get organized and take it one step at a time. To begin integrating and testing out restorative discipline within your MTSS right away, check out these strategies:

- **PREVENTION MATTERS.** Focus on evidence-based classroom or school universal design practices. This meets the needs of most students and prevents them from moving up the tiers. The most basic practice is building rapport with your students. Relationships = Prevention. So start working on those relationships!
    - Greet every student at your classroom door.
    - "Check in" emotionally with each student throughout the class period or day.
    - Provide student performance updates on a regular basis to establish trust and ensure students believe you are invested in their success.
- **ACCURATE ASSESSMENTS.** Learn more about your students' needs through accurate, proven assessments. Try Positive Youth Development's evidence-based assessment system, "40 Developmental Assets," which can be found online and is easy for students to take.
    - The assessments provide real insight into students' areas of need.

- The 40 Developmental Assets assessment provides students with a personalized self-evaluation tool.
- Students can begin to understand their own patterns and behaviors.
- **SCHOOLWIDE PROBLEM-SOLVING.** Identify significant data points around student need gaps, and analyze possible solutions.
  - What lessons are students struggling with?
  - When are students commonly going off-task?
  - Craft a plan to correct or support your instruction.
  - Develop a tracking system that works for you to evaluate your plan's effectiveness.
- **PARENTAL INVOLVEMENT.** If you haven't met or spoken directly with parents, you haven't "tried everything." When you meet with the parents, you won't get them on your side by telling them how horrible their child is. Show them you care about their child. Many more supportive and happy parents exist than not. You just don't hear much from the people who are happy.

> WHEN YOU MEET WITH THE PARENTS, YOU WON'T GET THEM ON YOUR SIDE BY TELLING THEM HOW HORRIBLE THEIR CHILD IS. SHOW THEM YOU CARE ABOUT THEIR CHILD.

- Commit to a schedule of calling parents at the end of the day. Start with two or three on your first day, and continue this routine until you've reached them all.

- Discuss the positive and negative patterns you've observed through the data you've collected and analyzed.

- Work together to keep your students on track toward success.

A BLUEPRINT FOR FULL IMPLEMENTATION

This Hack helps you make an outline, using restorative discipline, to create an MTSS model built around culture. In the same breath, you have to remember to adapt and identify personal solutions for students. What works for one student that day might not be effective for a different student on that same day. In fact, what works for one student today might not work for him tomorrow. The key is to be flexible and adaptable to the needs of students. The four essential components of MTSS are: screening, progress monitoring, multi-tiered support/preventive system, and data-based decision-making.

STEP 1: Screening.

Utilizing an evidence-based screening tool is essential to comprehensively meet student needs. Positive Youth Development offers the 40 Developmental Asset surveys to compartmentalize internal and external assets. Internal assets include commitment to learning, positive values, social competencies, and positive identity. External assets include empowerment, support, boundaries, expectations, and constructive use of time. The primary goal of this screening is to identify at-risk students and gaps in instruction.

The asset checklist demonstrates self-identified supports as well as gaps in support for a student. You can create schoolwide interventions by analyzing the most substantial student asset gaps.

> Example: If most of your students do not check boxes in the "Positive Values" section in the internal asset component, then develop self-esteem programs. One program could be a Men's Group, made up of just boys, that would work on creating a positive self-image.

To continue this process, create a mission statement for your school of what you hope to accomplish and capture through screening. Post this statement in a visible spot and communicate it to all stakeholders, including students, staff, parents, and community members. Also, prominently display the statement on your school website.

> Example: We believe in using restorative practices, supporting mental health and specific disability needs, motivating encouraging intrinsic systemic changes, and targeting soft-skill training to assist students throughout every aspect of their development.

Create an evidence-based and culturally responsive framework to improve student outcomes. This screening will also help you identify students who are at risk and need more help than the average child.

STEP 2: Progress monitoring.

Progress monitoring is essential for evaluating student support systems and responses to interventions. It also allows the educator to "pause" and reflect on the instruction, the students' growth or challenges, and the overall classroom culture. Likewise, it can allow students to reflect on their own growth, both academically and behaviorally.

To establish a progress monitoring system in your school, ask yourself what you need to track most closely. You might begin with where your school needs to improve, such as in attendance or tardiness. Other systems might focus on test results, depending on what improvements you want to make in your school's culture. Each week, consider progress monitoring:

- Attendance (compare to every period of the day)
    - Grade-level attendance
    - Teacher-by-teacher comparison
    - Tardiness
    - Grade-level tardiness
    - Tardiness by class hour
- Subject mastery
    - In-class testing
    - Formal standardized testing
    - Practice standardized testing
    - College or career placement testing

- Discipline

    - Number of referrals to the office

    - Number of suspensions (in and out of school)

    - Number of expulsions

    - Number of "repeat offenders"

    - Most common referral codes reported

Students can monitor their own progress through reflection sheets or short-essay responses. Consider asking students at the end of each week:

- What is one thing you did well this week?

- What is one thing you could have done better this week?

- What is one thing you hope to achieve by the end of next week?

- What is one behavior you are proud of this week?

- What is one behavior you wish you could re-do?

- What was your favorite moment this week, from school or at home?

Decide how often you want to conduct progress monitoring based on where the student falls in the tiers of support in the MTSS model. A student in Tier 1 may need progress monitoring only once per semester. A student in Tier 2 may need weekly or bi-weekly monitoring. The intensive Tier 3 student will most likely require daily to weekly monitoring. Come up with a system that works best! You will see more on this in the next Hack.

STEP 3: Multi-tiered support and preventive interventions.

Maintain multiple tiers in your system for the best prevention and attention to detail.

STEP 4: Data-based decision-making.

Analyze the progress monitoring to see what is effective and what is not. The more effective a program or intervention is, the more you should use it. If data shows that a certain strategy is not as effective with a certain subset of students, then adjust! Restorative practices can be both universal or intensive, but they are not a one-size-fits-all approach. Carefully analyze the trends in your data to meet the needs of every student.

To help, use online data assessment tools such as Conover Online. Many software companies also develop innovative apps for cell phones to help monitor, track, and analyze data.

Having systematic procedures for each tier of your MTSS model creates an easier implementation, which is important for tracking the model's recidivism and effectiveness. All staff must be consistent and committed to the mission of the MTSS model and the embedded restorative practices for this to truly work.

Consistency allows students to understand and accept how your school handles behaviors and the progressive factor of discipline. Though individual student predictability may change, giving all students a consistent set of expectations and tools will better equip them for success in school and in life.

OVERCOMING PUSHBACK

A multi-tiered system of supports requires a schoolwide understanding of restorative practices and for all staff to be on the same page. Some staff members might be resistant to these practices, or not fluent enough to be successful. Here are tips to overcome these obstacles:

WHAT I DO IN MY CLASSROOM WORKS. Some veteran teachers have been doing things their own way for many years. They already seem to have a good grasp on classroom management and the students are generally well-behaved in their rooms. Before implementing MTSS systems, it's important to get buy-in from those veteran teachers. Compliment them on what they already are doing effectively, but coach them toward a better way to handle incidents when things do get above basic classroom management. While they might be engaging in a good rapport with students, they are still surely going to come across negative behaviors. Tell them that they can use their great teacher-student relationships to not only coach them academically, but behaviorally. Remind them of the growth mindset and its applications to behavior.

EVERY KID SHOULD GET THE SAME PUNISHMENT. Each and every kid has different mechanics that make them tick. Differentiation in the classroom should not just be for academics. We need predictability in that students must take ownership of their actions and repair the harm, but we must use what we know about each student to determine the appropriate ways to do it. We must sell to stakeholders that students are getting consequences, and that those consequences are tailored to what is most effective for each student. Once students start to change their behaviors and take ownership for their actions, while also displaying better social-emotional skills, the results will speak for themselves.

BRING BACK DETENTIONS AND SUSPENSIONS. Patience will be key in implementing a multi-tiered system of supports. This system is not a quick fix. Instead of taking shortcuts, we are focusing on the long game. It is easy to revert back to punishing students, and it might feel good in the moment, but the instant gratification method of discipline will teach students to avoid punishment out of fear instead of internalizing the "why" behind meeting positive expectations. It will be key to be honest with your staff that the benefits of an MTSS might be slow to come, but will be better in the long run.

THE HACK IN ACTION

We have had a lot of great classes, and some not-so-great classes. We have continually wondered what we did in a prior life to deserve some of the classes we had, or if the guidance counselors that made the schedule were ticked off at us when they were assigning students to classes. We would routinely get stressed and anxious just thinking about the fact that Period 4 was coming next, right before lunch. Why couldn't the students in this class just be easier to manage like the other classes? Why do they care more about socializing than their work? We spent so much time redirecting students, even using sarcasm (a no-no), that we failed, almost daily, to accomplish what we were supposed to do. We chose to be combative with combative kids, which only reinforced that being combative was acceptable behavior. Don't do it!

The point of classroom management is to get students to act appropriately, not out of fear, but out of a desire to succeed. After several years of dealing with what we considered to be difficult classes, we decided something had to give. We reflected on how our own attitudes toward certain classes had inadvertently contributed to our classroom culture being what it was: a hot mess. As the saying goes, "When Mama ain't happy, ain't nobody happy."

While we were not their parents, we were certainly responsible for the culture of the classroom.

With that realization, we knew the next step: that we spent so much time planning the perfect lesson and hoping that it would be "enough," but we needed to change our focus and invest some of that time in planning how to *reach* kids. After all, we were there to teach students, not just teach content.

The first thing we did was get into the hallway before class started so we could greet the kids when they came in the door, sometimes even throwing in high-fives. We liked doing this so much that we realized that kids didn't even have to be our students for us to say hi to them, know their names, or ask how they were doing. In regard to the greetings, we didn't get as fancy as some teachers you see on social media, who have a personal handshake for each and every student, but we did our best.

We noticed an almost immediate change in the class. The kids seemed to be happy and more attentive when we started. "I'm glad you are here today" is something that all students love to hear, and it establishes belonging. The positive effect wore off after a little while into the class period, but this was a great start and we knew we were on to something.

Next, instead of calling out negative behaviors, such as "Get back to work," we started calling out the students who were doing the *right* thing. For example, "I like how Amber is being studious and using her resources." Lo and behold, the kids who were off-task also wanted to be recognized for being on-task.

While this worked for many kids, there were always exceptions. For students who needed more redirection than others, we always made sure to have three positive touch points for every negative interaction. We looked for ways to "catch them being good," figured out what their interests were, and made sure we always had non-academic conversations with them. For example, Charles had a major lack of motivation to do anything, often resulting in off-task behaviors instead of what he was supposed to be doing. Through our non-academic conversations with him, we realized that he loved video games. Although we hadn't played video games since we were in high school, for all Charles knew, we loved video games too. We would often ask him which games were best and what strategies he used in those games, to get him to engage with us.

After a couple of minutes of talking about video games, we could usually get him to do his work by either informing him that the more work he did in school, the more time he had to game, or by helping him find an interest in game design and keeping him motivated by doing what he needed to do to get into a game design program in college.

A major lesson that we learned was that students "should" just do their work, but that it rarely works that way. They aren't paid, they didn't choose to be there, and their brains aren't fully developed. This is why engagement and relationships matter! We must also sell the importance of what we are doing every day, and make sure kids know that we care about them.

These interventions for Tier 1 and Tier 2 students can be specialized and adjusted for students across the board, even those who require Tier 3-level interventions. Relationship-building and positive classroom management meet the needs of most students. We must always start there!

Meeting the needs of all your students in the form of high-quality classroom teaching and management is the most common preventive tool. Students may need additional support and accommodations to help them succeed, but delivering these things in a way that reaches *all* students is key. Restorative practices create a culture of success that can be facilitated in every tier of the MTSS model. Knowing your students' needs and having them identify their personal needs are the keys to creating data-driven decisions.

HACK 9

CREATE A SNAPSHOT
USE DATA TO TRACK BEHAVIORS, COACH STUDENTS, AND ADDRESS RECIDIVISM

Most of the world will make decisions by either guessing or using their gut. They will be either lucky or wrong.
—Suhail Doshi, founder, Mixpanel

THE PROBLEM: WE DON'T KNOW WHAT WE DON'T KNOW

MANY TEACHERS REPEATEDLY are frustrated by a lack of administrative support with some of their most difficult students. The same students get away with doing the same things on a daily or weekly basis, disrupting the learning environments of other students. Many teachers feel powerless when it comes to giving out consequences, or fear looking bad and being judged by their administrators if they ask for help or send a kid to the office. Other teachers feel that when they do send students down to the office or ask for help, nothing changes. Conversely, administrators hear from staff about the students who do whatever they want in the school because they are supposedly free to do so.

As an administrator, I often ask what steps teachers have taken to build relationships with those students and how they have partnered with parents to help the students grow. The next thing I do is review the log entries in our student information system to understand what infractions the student has incurred, where patterns exist, and the action steps taken to flip the student's behavior. I consider many questions, including: How many times has this student done this? What consistencies exist? How many other learners are exhibiting the same behavior? Are the expectations clear, is there any bias, is the teacher fixating on particular behaviors?

More often than not, the students have no track record of behaviors logged, the parents have not been contacted, and teachers cannot adequately explain the steps they have taken to build relationships with the students or correct the behaviors (beyond verbal warnings or calling them out). Sometimes those same students are having problems in other classrooms with other teachers, but due to a lack of evidence, teachers try to solve the problems by themselves rather than as collective units with other teachers, parents, and administration.

Proper record keeping is necessary for data to become actionable. Teachers need a user-friendly system that has the proper supports built-in, and is accessible to the right stakeholders. If systems are convoluted or nonexistent, teachers and staff members do not put in the effort to properly track student behaviors. Administrators cannot determine an actionable consequence for a student if no clear track record of classroom problems exists. Neither teachers nor administrators can be consistent and fair with discipline if a system is not in place to keep students accountable for their actions.

Teachers and administrators must have current and real-time data in order to effectively take action on correcting behaviors. A student who committed an infraction today will not likely learn from the mistake if corrective action occurs a week or more later.

For larger schools, this is not an easy feat, as administrators might have a lengthy list of disciplinary issues to address each day, multiple parents to contact, and a difficult time balancing their other responsibilities. School leaders must work in tandem with instructors to create a mutually beneficial system of support through data-tracking and restorative solutions.

THE HACK: CREATE A SNAPSHOT

In order for a school to maintain high expectations academically, emotionally, and behaviorally, it must have a clear, concise, and consistent vision for success. Students face different expectations, rules, policies, and consequences that change from classroom to classroom, teacher to teacher, and administrator to administrator. Inconsistency causes confusion, which creates a moving target of what success looks like. Students want to be successful, parents want to help students be successful, but everyone needs to know how.

Schools collaboratively must develop a schoolwide system for collecting and managing student behavior, as well as establishing schoolwide measures of success. This system needs to be easy to understand, easy to navigate, backed by best practices, and used consistently and fairly by all school employees.

Academic or behavioral expectations don't mean much unless:

- Students know what they are.
- Students know exactly how they are being measured.
- Students are being held accountable to them.

- Students receive feedback and coaching on them.

As educators, we often are either bombarded by too much data that we do not have time to use, or faced with a lack of reliable data. We usually have more data than we know what to do with when it comes to academic results and state tests, yet have insufficient data about the "why" behind the academic data. We know which students did well and which subgroups of students achieved at what level, and we even know exactly which questions were missed and by whom. But we often do not put attendance, behavior, motivation, home life, and other variables beside the academic data—which means we're not getting the full picture.

If your school does not have a tracking system, you need to create your own or purchase a platform that meets your needs. This will help you examine the frequency of behaviors among individuals and groups of students. A simple way to create your own system is through Google Sheets. In one document, create a tab for each of your classes. In the far left column, list your students. Create a column for the date, a description of the behavior, the consequence you gave, and any action steps you took. At the end of the week, review your data to determine the efficacy of your restorative practices.

WE OFTEN DO NOT PUT ATTENDANCE, BEHAVIOR, MOTIVATION, HOME LIFE, AND OTHER VARIABLES BESIDE THE ACADEMIC DATA—WHICH MEANS WE'RE NOT GETTING THE FULL PICTURE.

You may need someone with Google Sheets experience (or a collaborative online substitute) who can add cumulative levels or points that incur from infractions into one column, which leads to a multi-tiered system of supports of restorative actions. While Google Docs includes limitations, such as a lack of parent and student interface and the possibility that too many collaborators might wreak havoc on the document, it is a cheap and easy way to get started with your data-tracking prototyping. Google products are pretty intuitive, aiding even your most technologically challenged colleague.

Another option is for your school to purchase a behavioral tracking system. Several options exist, including BehaviorFlip, a program that the authors of this book developed along with a software engineer. This behavior management system focuses on students' social-emotional holistic journey. It tracks student behaviors; includes accounts for students, parents, teachers, and administrators; and helps to implement and facilitate restorative justice.

WHAT YOU CAN DO TOMORROW

It is a serious challenge to transition away from complete teacher autonomy in managing student behavior, but you can ease the tension in several ways. The following steps will be useful in creating a united front for combating negative student behaviors and promoting positive student behaviors.

- **IDENTIFY THE BEHAVIORS YOU OR THE STAFF WANT TO SEE FROM STUDENTS.** We spend a lot of time noticing behaviors that harm the learning environment, even though those behaviors make up a small fraction of all of the good things that are happening in a classroom or school. We must think about what makes a student, classroom, and school successful. What could the students be doing that would help themselves and others? Perhaps we should first examine and evaluate our school mission statement and school goals. What do we expect from our students, and what do we need to coach them toward, to make the vision statement and goals become a reality?

In doing so, we not only want to identify the academic components, such as being studious, but also focus on positive behaviors and social and emotional learning components that will help students open up to becoming studious. Examples of behaviors that might lead to success are: being respectful, responsible, persistent, involved, focused, kind, and safe (in words, actions, and relationships).

- **IDENTIFY THE MOST PROBLEMATIC BEHAVIORS.** Chances are, you will have an easy time identifying the behaviors that you believe to be barriers to success in the classroom and school. It is, after all, the talk in many staff lounges, staff meetings, or hallway conversations. While countless behaviors drive us nuts, it is important to focus on the behaviors that have the largest consequences on a positive classroom learning environment–academically, socially, and emotionally. While texting during class might be annoying, this is probably not the sole behavior that causes a student to fail her midterms.

An easy way to determine behaviors that have the biggest negative impact might be to take a look at the behaviors that were identified as critical for student *success*. For example, if your administration believes it is important for a student to be responsible, then a problematic behavior would be a lack of responsibility. Another example might be respect. A positive classroom environment needs respect, and the lack of it has a detrimental effect on the students as well as the classroom environment as a whole.

Long story short, you need to develop umbrella behaviors that can get more specific when developing the schoolwide or classroom system for tracking and managing behaviors. For example, an umbrella behavior might be "responsibility," and the specific items that might fall under that umbrella include no late work, and bringing supplies to class. An umbrella behavior might be "share the space effectively," and the specific items that fall under that umbrella could be not interrupting class to ask a friend for gum and then leaving that gum stuck to the carpet.

- **IDENTIFY A BEHAVIOR COMMITTEE OR TEAM.** Find a variety of stakeholders—staff members, administrators, and possibly even parents or students—and form a behavior team. Make sure this team has a solid understanding of student behaviors and gets acquainted with details around restorative discipline. It's important for this group to focus on how to coach students toward better behaviors instead of simply punishing them. This team will begin the process of synthesizing positive and negative behaviors that they want to track using data. They will also be the team that analyzes the data and makes action plans to help combat negative behaviors and promote positive behaviors.

  It is critical that this team is committed and dedicated to keeping up with best practices in discipline, attending meetings, and contributing to the group. A lot of committees start off strong and fizzle out, so it will be important to nominate a strong committee chair who is organized, efficient, and a good delegator.

A BLUEPRINT FOR FULL IMPLEMENTATION

Finding a way to actually implement and sustain a schoolwide system successfully will take a lot of work, patience, and revision. It's critical for key staff to be involved in the process and work through the bumps and bruises as a team, and it will be well worth it in the long run. Create a sustainable system for tracking data, as well as actually using the data for improvements, to get the most out of the process. The following steps will put you and your school on the pathway toward success.

STEP 1: Pilot your behavior tracking system.

Countless systems, programs, and initiatives out there fall flat on their faces, to the frustration of all involved, who spent countless hours in meetings, vetting the programs, and doing the research. One of the biggest reasons new initiatives fail is that they went too big, too soon, without an appropriate rollout plan. We recommend that you start small so you can flush the flaws and frustrations out before things get too big. Starting with a small group of teachers allows you to work out the kinks before you take the system schoolwide, at which point you'll have an entire school— and a board of directors—to deal with. Start with just a few classrooms, or even a single classroom, by simply tracking positive and negative behaviors. Ask stakeholders for feedback, and implement changes as necessary.

Evaluate the big-picture concerns of whether the tracking system does what it was meant to do and is user-friendly. Some students might get intensive levels of interventions way too quickly, some tracked behaviors might be too trivial, some behaviors that you need to track might not be included, and many other variables can come into play when first piloting the tracking system. It is easier to fix these basic mistakes in functionality or to identify what training staff needs (if a tracking system is purchased), if only a few teachers are piloting the system.

STEP 2: Use data to reflect and improve.

Letting history repeat itself is a common offense when it comes to student behavior. Behavior is often inaccurately recorded and the notes are not used effectively, even though behavior is one of the leading causes of success or failure in school. The same students who struggled last week with behavior still struggle this week. The same students who struggled last year with behavior often still struggle this year. The behaviors of students are often manifested symptoms of their upbringing, self-esteem, entitlement, disability, engagement in school, and many other factors. When the symptoms are not treated effectively, or at all, they continue to present and often worsen. Accurate tracking of behaviors of students (the symptoms) will not only help treat and identify the behaviors, it will also help educators get down to the root cause of the behaviors through restorative practices.

Set a predetermined time period with your Behavior Committee for meeting and examining behavior trends. For example, you might choose to meet monthly or every quarter.

Most schools focus, if they focus on behaviors at all, on just suspensions and expulsions. Your new data tracker, however, should be able to get down into more details. The minor behaviors, if left untreated, often lead to major behaviors. Look for instances of disrespect, being unprepared, being off-task, or other categories that you identified as major barriers to student success.

Take a look at which teachers are giving out more consequences, as well, and which teachers are recognizing students for positive behaviors most often. Are the teachers who use restorative discipline with fidelity reporting fewer minor behaviors? Are teachers who have a lack of rapport with students having the most problems? Are younger teachers not holding students accountable when they should be? One important factor for analysis is comparing the number of incidents logged and what those incident types are, for all subgroups. Bias in school happens daily, not just when suspensions or expulsions occur. These biases can be invisible to administrators or other stakeholders because they are not reported, but they are certainly not invisible to the students who feel discriminated against.

After analyzing the data, make an action plan. Determine the biggest offense in the school and identify action steps for how to improve it. For example, if your biggest offense is off-task behavior, do research and work with your committee for solutions to decrease that problem. One example might be giving teachers tips on how to better monitor their rooms, such as leading from their feet instead of their seat during work time. Or having students close their laptop screens halfway or more when the teacher is talking so that the teacher knows that the students are not distracted. One big identified problem might be a lack of engaging instruction, resulting in students who do not care about the work.

Regardless of the root causes of the behaviors, having the data is important, and coming up with action plans is critical. If your staff members are giving consequences to a much higher percentage of a certain subgroup at your school, it might be time to look into cultural competency training, so teachers better understand the diverse students in their classrooms and are better aware of their own biases.

OVERCOMING PUSHBACK

Students might have difficulty adjusting to a system that holds them accountable for the same expectations in every part of the building because they can no longer get away with certain things, or pin teacher against teacher. Parents might feel that teachers are targeting their children for behaviors that other students are getting away with. Having data will help administrators keep teachers honest, help teachers keep students honest, and give parents a more defined glimpse into the behavioral struggles that inhibit academic achievement. Before they agree, though, expect pushback.

THIS MIGHT HURT MY RELATIONSHIPS WITH STUDENTS. It is possible to have good relationships with students and also hold them accountable for their actions and academics. There is a difference between being their friend and being their teacher. A teacher's job is to set optimal conditions for students to help them be successful. Sometimes, this includes tough love. No teacher loves having to record instances of a student being disrespectful or tardy, but students need to know that you mean business and are doing what it takes to help them be successful, as well as maintaining a positive and safe learning environment. Always preview and warn before assigning consequences, and keep it as positive as possible, but keep in mind that students need accountability. As long as you don't hold a grudge and you give students a fresh start tomorrow with how you treat them, they will bounce back and even want to live up to your expectations and not disappoint you.

I CARE ABOUT WHAT THE STUDENT DOES IN MY CLASS, NOT OTHER CLASSES. A key to implementing a tracking system to help reinforce positive behaviors, while also monitoring and coaching students on negative behaviors, is seeing the student on a broader level. For example, you might see that a student has an A in math, but to better understand the overall academic success of that student, it would be helpful to know how he is doing in English, history, science, and electives.

Think of a schoolwide data tracker as comparable to a GPA, reporting on the overall behavioral health of a student, while also giving you the ability to take a unique look into each classroom for each student to identify where the student is struggling. Once a school has a united front for combating negative behaviors, educators will be able to use patterns and trends in student behavior to create real change. If a student is chronically tardy to all classes, it can be fixed more quickly than when teachers have different ways of dealing with tardies, the teachers don't know about the tardies in the other classes, or some teachers don't worry about tardies. Instead, imagine that one student has been tardy to three different classes that day, and has been tardy numerous other times that week. When all of those tardies are tracked together, the student can receive corrective action after hitting a threshold established by the system, and take accountability for his or her actions.

TEACHERS DON'T HAVE ENOUGH TIME TO DO THIS. Lesson plans, emails, seating charts, grading, and the laundry list of other items teachers must accomplish often make them think just one more thing will break them. We keep on giving teachers more and more expectations and tasks, but often do not take anything off their plates. Teachers either revert to the easy button and kick students out of class and assign them a detention, or do nothing at all because they don't want to fill out the report or call home. Punishing kids before you figure out what is triggering their behavior solves nothing. If they know you want to know what is going on with them, and are conversational, your chance of success increases exponentially.

Building relationships with students and parents includes a lot of frontloading, but it actually saves time in the long run. Think how often and how much time you spend on discipline, distractions, tardies, and tracking down missing work. If we spent more time getting to know students and their triggers, we would spend less time dealing with their behaviors. We must keep in mind as educators that we are all on the same team, and our team should also include parents. Parents might be in denial about their child's wrongdoing, and it might take extra time to meet with parents, but put in the effort anyway. Once you have built a relationship with a parent through positive conversations about their child, the parent is usually more receptive to working with you on behavioral problems.

If behaviors still persist, managing and tracking those behaviors will get students the help they need to take corrective action, learn from their mistakes, and build empathy. Behaviors left undocumented and undealt with will worsen over time, and punishing behaviors without coaching will simply teach students to live in a carrot-and-stick system where they don't truly change for the betterment of themselves and others. Investing time in growing students through coaching and enforcing restorative justice will lead to fewer headaches later and better student citizens in your classroom.

THE HACK IN ACTION

Having a way to track behaviors, both positive and negative, empowers staff members to hold students accountable, while also building the skill sets needed for students to succeed.

Purdue Polytechnic High School in Indianapolis, Indiana, is a unique school in that students do not have a set bell schedule for the semester. In fact, the bell schedule changes weekly based on student needs and what is going on that week academically and with field trips or other special events. Students spend at least half of their week in personal learning time, where they move at their own pace on academic content, utilizing the curriculum placed on their learning management system. During personalized learning time, students can choose which area of the school to work in. If they need math help, they go to the Quant Lab. If they need science help, they go to the Science Lab. If they need help in English or history, they go to the Comms Lab.

While it is great to empower students to take ownership of their learning, make their own schedule, and prioritize their time, it is also a chance for students to showcase a plethora of unfortunate behaviors. We all have heard the phrase, "Give someone an inch and they'll take a mile," and that is exactly what some students chose to do with so much freedom. Teachers were seemingly spending more time redirecting students and dealing with behavior problems than actually coaching students on academic content. Some teachers felt powerless because they did not have an effective mechanism to hold students accountable for their behaviors, sometimes leading to high frustration levels.

At my prior school, I digitized an effective behavior tracking system to make tracking and managing behavior visible and cohesive among all staff, and to hold students accountable for their actions. I created a Google Doc, titled "BehaviorNet," that became the go-to spot for staff to log minor behaviors. This was successful once all staff members became fluent in how it worked. When I saw that teachers were struggling to manage student behavior, I showed what I had used at my previous school to a few teachers, with mixed reviews. Some teachers wanted to implement it the next day, some were reserved about seeking out negative behaviors, and others saw it as "something else we now have to do."

After prototyping the behavior management tracker, BehaviorNet, during summer school, more teachers saw the usefulness of having a way to monitor and track student behaviors. BehaviorNet was launched in the fall after summer school, and made a marked difference in student behaviors. Let's take a hypothetical student named David. David has problems going where he needs to go, staying where he needs to be, and keeping on-task. Every time David goes to a new space and is tardy or off-task, the teacher gives him a preview, a warning, and a consequence by logging the incident into the behavior management system. By the end of the day, David has received three different log entries by three different teachers. David still does not learn from his behaviors and continues with similar behaviors for the rest of the week.

The dean looks at the behavior management document and sees that David has accumulated eight log entries this week, primarily for off-task behavior and tardiness. In many schools, David has not done something "terrible enough" to warrant an office referral, so he might go on continuing his behavior without any interventions. But the dean realizes that these numerous minor behaviors are causing David to be unsuccessful while also frustrating teachers. The dean brings David in for a restorative intervention to build empathy for those affected by his actions, and how it causes him problems, and helps David make a plan for improvement.

As it turns out, David actually had a hard time figuring out what to do in his online work and how to manage his time, and had reverted to avoidance as a coping mechanism rather than seeking help from his teachers. As a result of the meeting, David better understood his options and improved his academic success.

To achieve a successful multi-tiered system of supports, your data must be readily available to continually analyze. If a school uses an effective electronic system to track data, staff will have less paperwork, make decisions more quickly, and have more time to focus on academics. The most important data is not just about improving proficiency on standards or lowering the number of discipline infractions. It reflects how many students:

- Feel loved
- Had breakfast that morning
- Feel supported
- Are happy
- Have hope

While the discipline data will be extremely useful in targeting behaviors and holding kids accountable, be sure you get to know the story behind the data before doling out consequences. Once we get to the root cause of the behaviors, we can enact lasting change with students.

Schools need to promote positive behaviors and combat negative behaviors as a cohesive unit. Creating a positive culture where students are treated equitably while also receiving coaching on behaviors requires proper reporting, effective execution of restorative practices, and analyzing behavioral data. We must pay careful attention to the behaviors that are not quantified by referrals, suspensions, and expulsions. We have numerous committees that revolve around academics and extracurriculars, but few schools have a committee that focuses on behavior data, even though behaviors are often one of the biggest strains on a school. We must identify disproportionality, provide professional development, and enact action plans to properly serve all students. We must get staff and stakeholders on board to see the long-term benefits of coaching students instead of punishing them.

CONCLUSION
STUDENTS NEED TO BE HEARD AND UNDERSTOOD

S TUDENTS ARE NOT inherently troubled. We must dive into behavior as we do any learning deficiency in the classroom. When we identify that the old carrot-and-stick discipline philosophies actually create more opposition, exclusion, and labeling, we can begin to truly address this rising epidemic. Restorative practices take incidents that would otherwise result in punishment and create recognition of behaviors, an obligation to repair the harm they caused, and action steps in making the wrong right. Emotional regulation isn't taught; it's learned.

Students are not adults. They need help with time management, study skills, prioritizing tasks, social skills, and character development. Instead of assuming immaturity or irresponsibility, assume they need coaching. We need to focus on supporting students who are not polished emotionally. This is why they need someone like you—to help them grow. Don't get mad at kids if they aren't problem-solving. Teach them how to do it, over and over. Many adults still need help problem-solving. Communication is *tough*. Students need to be heard if they're going to learn successful conflict resolution skills. Preaching what is "right" to students does not reach them.

To grow, students need coaching, modeling, and consistency in expectations. It is quick and easy to punish students for minor behaviors, but it rarely leads to long-term change. Most students do not cognitively think out their actions in full; this is a fact. They are impulsive and often do not understand the implications of their actions. We must help them want to do the right thing and to think extrinsically. We must be intentional about teaching students the skills they need to be successful, but even more so, redirecting them when they make a mistake so they know what they should have done to be successful. If you want to change kids' behavior, look for instances when they are doing the right thing, and praise them. When students demonstrate empathy, praise and affirmation will help them replicate it. Suspending students is like giving them a locked door and no key. Restorative practices mean giving students the key to not only stay out of trouble, but to unlock their potential to achieve. The best way to help students learn from a mistake is not to get rid of them, berate them, or put them in a detention, but to have them make it right. Punishment might be quick and easy, but the Band-Aid effect is short-term. Restorative practices take effort, but the effects are long-term. We have two choices: try to correct behavior by continuing to punish, or spend time building relationships, getting down to the root of issues, and helping students repair the harm they caused.

Perhaps one of the most valuable traits we can teach our students is how to feel empathy. Empathy is not shaming students or making them feel bad, but teaching them to understand those who have been affected by their actions, as well as the need to repair the harm. For example, if a student throws food in the cafeteria, the logical consequence would be for the student to clean the cafeteria and make it right with the cafeteria staff and custodians. On their own, students might simply see food on a table or on the ground, but not see how it affects others. Students grow up in a self-centered society where impulse and the "in the now" moments often drive actions, versus thinking before acting and reflecting upon their actions afterward.

It doesn't matter how good a plan, program, or vision is if you don't have investment and input from others. Restorative practices do not just happen; they are activities that all of your education stakeholders believe are best for students. A school community behind restorative practices can help launch your school into a world of fewer suspensions and expulsions, increased student achievement, and an amazing and collaborative school culture. We all want to be part of creating an environment where others are happy to work; where parents are happy to send their kids; and most important, where kids feel safe, empowered, and want to learn. Restorative practices can make that happen—and improve everyone's lives at the same time.

MEET THE AUTHORS

 **NATHAN MAYNARD** works as an administrator at Purdue Polytechnic High School in Indianapolis, as the dean of culture. He is the co-founder of BehaviorFlip, a restorative behavior management system that helps build a culture of empathy and responsibility. Nathan studied behavioral neuroscience at Purdue University. He has been facilitating restorative practices for over ten years in a wide range of educational settings, and working with at-risk populations. He was awarded Youth Worker of the Year for dedicating his time to helping underserved and underprivileged youth involved with the juvenile justice system.

Nathan is passionate about addressing the school-to-prison pipeline crisis and closing the achievement gap by implementing trauma-informed behavioral practices. He has expertise in dialectical behavioral coaching, motivational interviewing, positive youth development, restorative justice, and trauma-informed building practices to assist with creating positive school climates. Connect with him on Twitter @NmaynardEdu.

BRAD WEINSTEIN works as an administrator at the Purdue Polytechnic High School Network in Indianapolis as the director of curriculum and instruction. He is the co-founder of BehaviorFlip, a restorative behavior management system that helps build a culture of empathy and responsibility. Brad is the creator of @teachergoals, one of the most popular educational accounts in the world on Twitter, Facebook, and Instagram.

He served as principal for two years at Irvington Preparatory Academy on the east side of Indianapolis. Brad also worked as a coach and STEM department chair, and won Teacher of the Year in 2016 as a science teacher at Zionsville West Middle School in Whitestown, Indiana. While at Zionsville, he was one of the first teachers in the nation to implement a version of genius hour that worked within state standards, giving students voice and choice to pursue their science interests with student-led projects. Connect with him on Twitter @WeinsteinEdu.

MORE FROM
TIMES 10 BOOKS

HACKING EDUCATION
10 Quick Fixes For Every School

By Mark Barnes (@markbarnes19) & Jennifer Gonzalez (@cultofpedagogy)

In the award-winning first Hack Learning Series book, *Hacking Education*, Mark Barnes and Jennifer Gonzalez employ decades of teaching experience and hundreds of discussions with education thought leaders to show you how to find and hone the quick fixes that every school and classroom need. Using a Hacker's mentality, they provide **one Aha moment after another** with 10 Quick Fixes For Every School—solutions to everyday problems and teaching methods that any teacher or administrator can implement immediately.

"Barnes and Gonzalez don't just solve problems; they turn teachers into hackers—a transformation that is right on time."

—DON WETTRICK, AUTHOR OF *PURE GENIUS*

HACKING PROJECT BASED LEARNING
10 Easy Steps to PBL and Inquiry in the Classroom

By Ross Cooper (@rosscoops31) and Erin Murphy (@murphysmusings5)

As questions and mysteries around PBL and inquiry continue to swirl, experienced classroom teachers and school administrators Ross Cooper and Erin Murphy have written a book that will empower those intimidated by PBL to cry, "I can do this!" while at the same time providing added value for those who are already familiar with the process. Impacting teachers and leaders around the world, *Hacking Project Based Learning* demystifies what PBL is all about with **10 hacks that construct a simple path** that educators and students can easily follow to achieve success. Forget your prior struggles with project based learning. This book makes PBL an amazing gift you can give all students tomorrow!

"*Hacking Project Based Learning* is a classroom essential. Its ten simple 'hacks' will guide you through the process of setting up a learning environment in which students will thrive from start to finish."

—DANIEL H. PINK, *NEW YORK TIMES* BESTSELLING AUTHOR OF *DRIVE*

HACKING ASSESSMENT
10 Ways To Go Gradeless In a Traditional Grades School
By Starr Sackstein (@mssackstein)

In the bestselling *Hacking Assessment,* award-winning teacher and world-renowned formative assessment expert Starr Sackstein unravels one of education's oldest mysteries: How to assess learning without grades—even in a school that uses numbers, letters, GPAs, and report cards. While many educators can only muse about the possibility of a world without grades, teachers like Sackstein are **reimagining education**. In this unique, eagerly-anticipated book, Sackstein shows you exactly how to create a remarkable no-grades classroom like hers, a vibrant place where students grow, share, thrive, and become independent learners who never ask, "What's this worth?"

"The beauty of the book is that it is not an empty argument against grades—but rather filled with valuable alternatives that are practical and will help to refocus the classroom on what matters most."

—ADAM BELLOW, WHITE HOUSE PRESIDENTIAL INNOVATION FELLOW

HACKING LEADERSHIP
10 Ways Great Leaders Inspire Learning That Teachers, Students, and Parents Love

By Joe Sanfelippo (@joe_sanfelippo) and Tony Sinanis (@tonysinanis)

In the runaway bestseller *Hacking Leadership,* internationally known school leaders Joe Sanfelippo and Tony Sinanis bring readers inside schools that few stakeholders have ever seen—places where students not only come first but have a unique voice in teaching and learning. Sanfelippo and Sinanis ignore the bureaucracy that stifles many leaders, focusing instead on building a culture of **engagement, transparency and, most important, fun**. *Hacking Leadership* has superintendents, principals, and teacher leaders around the world employing strategies they never before believed possible and learning how to lead from the middle. Want to revolutionize teaching and learning at your school or district? *Hacking Leadership* is your blueprint. Read it today, energize teachers and learners tomorrow!

"The authors do a beautiful job of helping leaders focus inward, instead of outward. This is an essential read for leaders who are, or want to lead, learner-centered schools."

—GEORGE COUROS, AUTHOR OF *THE INNOVATOR'S MINDSET*

HACKING SCHOOL CULTURE
Designing Compassionate Classrooms

By Angela Stockman (@angelastockman) and Ellen Feig Gray (@ellenfeiggray)

Bullying prevention and character-building programs are deepening our awareness of how today's kids struggle and how we might help, but many agree: They aren't enough to create school cultures where students and staff flourish. This inspired Angela Stockman and Ellen Feig Gray to begin seeking out systems and educators who were getting things right. Their experiences taught them that the real game changers are using a human-centered approach. Inspired by other design thinkers, many teachers are creating learning environments where seeking a greater understanding of themselves and others is the highest standard. They're also realizing that compassion is best cultivated in the classroom, not the boardroom or the auditorium. It's here that we learn how to pull one another close. It's here that we begin to negotiate the distances between us, too.

"Hacking School Culture: Designing Compassionate Classrooms is a valuable addition to the Hack Learning Series. It provides concrete support and suggestions for teachers to improve their interactions with their students at the same time they enrich their own professional experiences. Although primarily aimed at K–12 classrooms, the authors' insightful suggestions have given me, a veteran college professor, new insights into positive classroom dynamics which I have already begun to incorporate into my classes."

—Louise Hainline, Ph.D., Professor of Psychology, Brooklyn College of CUNY

HACKING EARLY LEARNING

10 Building Blocks to Success in Pre-K–3 That All Teachers and School Leaders Should Know

By Jessica Cabeen (@jessicacabeen)

School readiness, closing achievement gaps, partnering with families, and innovative learning are just a few of the reasons the early learning years are the most critical years in a child's life. In what ways have schools lost the critical components of early learning—preschool through third grade—and how can we intentionally bring those ideas and instructional strategies back? In *Hacking Early Learning*, kindergarten school leader, early childhood education specialist, and Minnesota State Principal of the Year Jessica Cabeen provides strategies for teachers, principals, and district administrators for best practices in preschool through third grade, including connecting these strategies to all grade levels.

"Jessica Cabeen is not afraid to say she's learned from her mistakes and misconceptions. But it is those mistakes and misconceptions that qualify her to write this book, with its wonderfully user-friendly format. For each problem specified, there is a hack and actionable advice presented as "What You Can Do Tomorrow" and "A Blueprint for Full Implementation." Jessica's leadership is informed by both head and heart and, because of that, her wisdom will be of value to those who wish to teach and lead in the early childhood field."

—Rae Pica, Early Childhood Education Keynote Speaker and Author of *What If Everybody Understood Child Development?*

Adam Chamberlin & Svetoslav Matejic

UNDERSTANDING APATHY,
ENGAGEMENT, AND MOTIVATION
IN THE CLASSROOM

QUIT POINT:
Understanding Apathy, Engagement, and Motivation in the Classroom

By Adam Chamberlin and Svetoslav Matejic (@pomme_ed)

Two classroom teachers grew tired of apathy in their classrooms, so they asked two simple but crucial questions: Why do students quit? And more important, what should we do about it? In *Quit Point: Understanding Apathy, Engagement, and Motivation in the Classroom*, authors Chamberlin and Matejic present a new way of approaching those issues. The Quit Point—their theory on how, why, and when people quit and how to stop quitting before it happens—will **transform how teachers reach the potential of each and every student.**

Quit Point reveals how to confront apathy and build student engagement; interventions to challenge students to keep going; and how to experience a happier, more fulfilling, teaching experience—starting tomorrow. Researchers, school leaders, and teachers have wondered for centuries what makes students stop working. Now, the answer is finally here. Read *Quit Point* today and stop quitting in your school or class before it begins.

HACKING ENGAGEMENT
50 Tips & Tools to Engage Teachers and Learners Daily
By James Alan Sturtevant (@jamessturtevant)

Some students hate your class. Others are just bored. Many are too nice, or too afraid, to say anything about it. Don't let it bother you; it happens to the best of us. But now, it's **time to engage!** In *Hacking Engagement*, the seventh book in the Hack Learning Series, veteran high school teacher, author, and popular podcaster James Sturtevant provides 50—that's right five-oh—tips and tools that will engage even the most reluctant learners daily. Sold in dozens of countries around the world, *Hacking Engagement* has become an educator's go-to guide for better student engagement in all grades and subjects. In fact, this book is so popular, Sturtevant penned a follow-up, *Hacking Engagement Again*, which brings 50 more powerful strategies. Find both at HackLearningBooks.com.

HACKING DIGITAL LEARNING STRATEGIES

10 Ways to Launch EdTech Missions in Your Classroom

By Shelly Sanchez Terrell (@ShellTerrell)

In this breakthrough book, international EdTech presenter and NAPW Woman of the Year Shelly Sanchez Terrell demonstrates the power of EdTech Missions—lessons and projects that inspire learners to use web tools and social media to innovate, research, collaborate, problem-solve, campaign, crowd fund, crowdsource, and publish. The 10 Missions in *Hacking DLS* are more than enough to transform how teachers integrate technology, but there's also much more here. Included in the book is a **38-page Mission Toolkit**, complete with reproducible mission cards, badges, polls, and other handouts that you can copy and distribute to students immediately.

"The secret to Shelly's success as an education collaborator on a global scale is that she shares information most revered by all educators, information that is original, relevant, and vetted, combining technology with proven education methodology in the classroom. This book provides relevance to a 21st-century educator."

—THOMAS WHITBY, AUTHOR, PODCASTER, BLOGGER, CONSULTANT, CO-FOUNDER OF #EDCHAT

HACKING CLASSROOM MANAGEMENT

10 Ideas To Help You Become the Type of Teacher They Make Movies About

By Mike Roberts (@baldroberts)

Utah English Teacher of the Year and sought-after speaker Mike Roberts brings you 10 quick and easy classroom management hacks that will **make your classroom the place to be** for all your students. He shows you how to create an amazing learning environment that actually makes discipline, rules, and consequences obsolete, no matter if you're a new teacher or a 30-year veteran teacher.

"Mike writes from experience; he's learned, sometimes the hard way, what works and what doesn't, and he shares those lessons in this fine little book. The book is loaded with specific, easy-to-apply suggestions that will help any teacher create and maintain a classroom where students treat one another with respect, and where they learn."

—CHRIS CROWE, ENGLISH PROFESSOR AT BYU, PAST PRESIDENT OF ALAN, AUTHOR OF *DEATH COMING UP THE HILL, GETTING AWAY WITH MURDER: THE TRUE STORY OF THE EMMETT TILL CASE; MISSISSIPPI TRIAL, 1955*

HACKING THE WRITING WORKSHOP
Redesign with Making in Mind

By Angela Stockman (@AngelaStockman)

Agility matters. This is what Angela Stockman learned when she left the classroom over a decade ago to begin supporting young writers and their teachers in schools. What she learned transformed her practice and led to the publication of her primer on this topic: *Make Writing: 5 Teaching Strategies that Turn Writer's Workshop Into a Maker Space.* Now, Angela is back with more stories from the road and **plenty of new thinking to share.** In *Make Writing*, Stockman upended the traditional writing workshop by combining it with the popular ideas that drive the maker space. Now, she is expanding her concepts and strategies and breaking new ground in *Hacking the Writing Workshop.*

"Good writing is good thinking. This is a book about how to think better, for yourself and with others."

—DAVE GRAY, FOUNDER OF XPLANE, AND AUTHOR OF *THE CONNECTED COMPANY, GAMESTORMING,* AND *LIMINAL THINKING*